the Ultimate season

BULLS TAKE IT ALL

Bonus Books, Inc., Chicago

© 1996 by Bonus Books, Inc.

00 99 98 97 96   5 4 3 2 1

Library of Congress Catalog Card Number: 96-85406

International Standard Book Number: 1-56625-072-2

Bonus Books, Inc.
160 East Illinois Street
Chicago, Illinois 60611

All photos courtesy of NBA. Reprinted with permission of the copyright owner.

Cover and interior design by Richmond A. Jones.

Printed in the United States of America

Contents

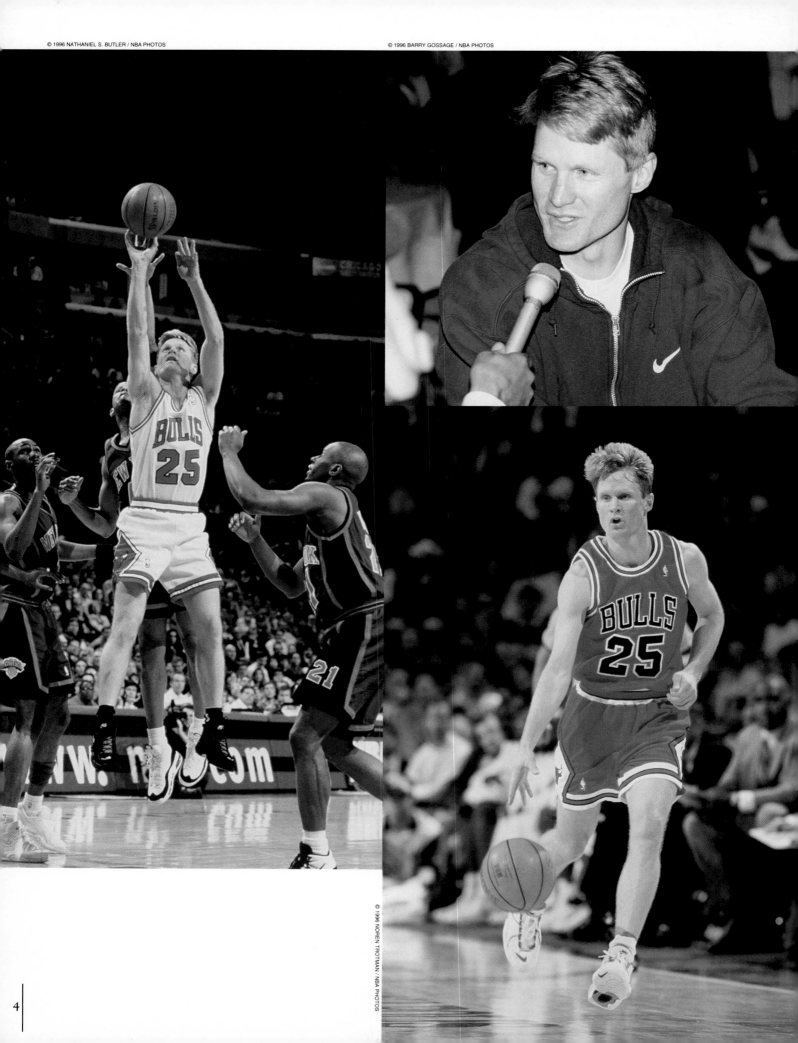

Steve Kerr

"The journey is the reward"

Sitting in a chair in the film room of the Berto Center, I looked around. The players were all filing in as 10:00 a.m. approached. In a few minutes Phil Jackson and his staff would walk in and discuss the strategy for Game 2 of the NBA Finals versus the Sonics. This was our usual routine on game day throughout the season. We would watch film of our opponent, discuss a game plan, and then head down to the floor for a light practice.

It's a family affair. Steve Kerr and his three-year-old son Nicholas celebrate the NBA championship in the Bulls locker room.

5

As I waited for the meeting to start, I couldn't help thinking about how close we were to winning the NBA Championship. Three more wins! Three more wins and we would be able to enjoy the traditional rite of all championship winning professional sports teams — the locker room champagne celebration! As a sports fan from the time I was old enough to walk I had marvelled at dozens of championship celebrations. Super Bowl victors, World Series winners, NBA champions — every year I watched the look of utter joy on the faces of these grown men as they broke down crying, dousing each other with champagne. To me that was the coolest thing in the world. I would have done *anything* to experience a scene like that.

So here I was daydreaming of being a part of that climactic moment when Phil walked in and started our meeting. "Fellas," he began, "I want you to look on the bulletin board in the back of the room and tell me if you see the quote I hung up." We craned our necks to see what he was talking about, but Toni Kukoc was the only one close enough, so Phil asked Toni to read it. "It says, 'the journey is the reward,' coach," he replied. Phil repeated it. "The journey is the reward." (It was a quote from a book Phil had given all of us the previous year — *The Little Zen Handbook*.) "What that means is that if we can win three more games and become NBA champions, our reward is not necessarily a ring or a playoff check or a locker room celebration, but the joy of the journey itself. And the journey is not over yet."

Phil moved on and began to talk about the night's game plan, but I sat and pondered his message for a moment. He was right. What I would one day remember from this season would go well beyond a ring ceremony or a locker room champagne celebration. I would remember the thousands of steps it took to complete the journey. The frustrating loss to the Magic in last year's playoffs. The off-season conditioning to prepare for this year. The rigors of training camp. The hundreds of hours spent on the practice floor, the film room, and the weight room. The midnight charter flights to take us to the next game. And most of

all, experiencing these moments with all my teammates. Yes, Phil was right. Three more wins would mean a championship. But it would also mean the completion of one of the most thrilling journeys of our lives.

Where did it start? I believe the journey began the moment Michael returned to the Bulls on March 17, 1995. For the previous season and three-quarters of the next one, we had failed to develop into a serious championship contender without Michael. We were good, but not good enough. With the news of Michael's return, however, we knew we were right back in the hunt. We immediately righted a season that had gone astray, winning 13 of the final 17 games of the season. We headed to the playoffs with a strange sort of confidence. We hadn't played together for much more than a month, and we lacked the sort of unity that more time together would have provided. Still, we had Michael. We had Scottie Pippen. We had Toni Kukoc. We knew we had enough talent to make a run.

After beating a good Charlotte team in the first round, we headed to Orlando to play the Magic. They were a young team that had never advanced past the first round of the playoffs, and we knew we had the experience factor on our side. We wanted to get the first game of the series to really put some doubt in their minds and to wrestle the homecourt advantage away.

We played a very good Game 1, taking advantage of Orlando's mistakes and controlling the game most of the way. We had the ball and a one-point lead with 18 seconds left. And then it happened. Michael dribbled the ball into the front court, waiting for the inevitable foul that would stop the clock for the Magic and send him to the free-throw line. But as he crossed halfcourt he lost sight of Nick Anderson, who sneaked behind him and deftly poked the ball away. Penny Hardaway recovered the loose ball and delivered it to Horace Grant for an easy dunk and the game was over.

We eventually lost the series in six games, and our season came to a shocking close. Just as quickly as Michael had returned in March, our season had disappeared. And all anyone could talk about was Game 1 of the series. "How could Michael have the ball stolen from him?" people asked. "It never would have happened in his prime," they cried. "He's over the hill. He doesn't have it anymore. He shouldn't have come back." I must have seen the replay of the steal 100 times after it happened.

I couldn't believe it. Never mind that Michael had scored 42 points in Game 2 to even the series at one apiece. Never mind the 40 he had to beat Charlotte in the opening game of the play-offs. Or the 55 he scored in Madison Square Garden to beat the Knicks in April. Forget the fact that he averaged 26 points a game for us and carried us whenever we struggled. The fans and media still believed, almost unanimously, that he wasn't the same guy. And, despite the fact that a lack of rebounding was the obvious reason for our loss to Orlando, people were quick to place the blame on Michael.

As is our custom, each player met individually with Phil and Jerry Krause at the conclusion of the season. We were all asked what we thought we needed to do to return to the form that had won three titles for the Bulls earlier in the decade. It was at that point that our mission for this season began. The players began to work out, and management began to plan. We all agreed that with a year under our belts playing together, we would be a much stronger unit. Still, we had to make some strategic moves. To defeat Orlando, whom we knew we'd have to beat to reach the Finals, we had to be able to rebound, and we had to be able to defend their big guards.

Management's first step was to get Ron Harper back in the mix. He was coming off a wasted season in which he found himself on the bench and uncomfortable with his position in the offense. Still, he was a big guard with long arms who could definitely defend and score on the fast break. Ron had averaged over 20 points a game earlier in his career with Cleveland and the Clippers, so he had plenty of ability. Phil told Ron in their meeting that he wanted him to really work hard over the summer, because he planned to start him.

Still, there was the question of rebounding. Toni Kukoc had played out of position at the power forward spot, and rebounding was not his forte. He was a fabulous perimeter player with the size and skills to create matchup problems for nearly everyone. Because of this versatility Phil wanted to bring him off the bench, so he could plug him into any one of four positions. That would provide a huge scoring burst off the bench and free Toni from the physical responsibilities of a starting power forward in the NBA. Even though Toni wanted to start, Phil talked to him about the importance of bench players. He used Kevin McHale of the Celtics as an example of someone who didn't start, but was still an All-Star player. Whether Toni would accept that role and flourish as a sixth man remained to be seen, but Phil was convinced it was the right move.

Then came the hard part. Who could he plug into the starting power forward spot to provide the defense and rebounding that was ultimately so crucial to our success? Dickey Simpkins and Corey Blount were too young and inexperienced to immediately take over. Both had promise but needed a few years to blossom. Unfortunately, the Bulls didn't have the luxury to wait that long, so the answer was either to sign a free agent or make a trade. The free agent market was thin and unimpressive, and to trade for someone who could make a big difference meant giving up one of our best players. It seemed to be a hopeless situation.

That, of course, was when Jerry Krause and Phil Jackson made "the gamble." A trade was engineered to send Will Perdue to the Spurs for Dennis Rodman. Of all the players in the league the Bulls could have acquired, they took Rodman? The ultra-conservative Bulls trading for the enigmatic, controversial former Bad Boy rival from the Pistons? When I heard the news, I was shocked. Many questions immediately entered my mind; how would Dennis get along with Michael and Scottie? How would he fit into the triangle offense? How would Phil deal with Dennis' explosive personality that ultimately led to his dismissal from San Antonio? Would he tear our team apart?

The one question that never entered my mind, of course, was whether or not Dennis was the answer to our defensive and rebounding woes. We had just acquired the best rebounder in the league, and a first team all-defensive player. He was obviously perfect for us on paper. But would the whole thing work? I wondered about that, but the more I thought about the trade the more I liked it. Why not? We weren't going to win the championship the way our team was constituted before, and we had no other viable options. Putting Dennis in our lineup all of a sudden completed the picture, assuming of course that he could become a part of the team and keep himself under control. With Phil's coaching style and the strong personality of the team, I felt we could pull it off.

So we started training camp in October with a lot of talent and expectations, but also quite a bit of uncertainty. Dennis arrived and barely said a word for a month. Michael battled his way through camp with the eyes of the basketball world upon him, waiting for him to fail. Ron Harper tried to regain the form that had made him a top NBA player for many years but had eluded him the previous season. The rest of us worked and watched and anticipated. None of us really knew what to expect.

It seemed like everyone else expected us to dominate the NBA. One day during training camp we all saw Bill Walton on NBC saying that he expected us to be one of the great teams of all time. Another day someone brought a copy of the *Sun-Times* in which beat writer Lacy Banks predicted we would win 70 games. I remember looking at Jud Buechler and asking, "Could we really be that good?" He just shrugged as if to say, "Who knows?"

The many questions that we had entering the season were answered very quickly. Was Michael better after a summer of heavy training? Forty-one points in the opener (a win over

Charlotte) seemed to be a pretty good answer. Was Dennis the power forward we needed? After a calf injury shelved him for two and a half weeks in November, he came back and immediately established himself as the leading rebounder in the league. Was Ron Harper confident as a starting guard in our lineup? He wasn't the scorer he once was, but his leg strength and conditioning were clearly much improved after a summer of hard work. He seemed to be fitting in nicely. Finally, what about Toni's return to the bench? He wasn't exactly happy about it, but Phil was thrilled to have his versatility and explosiveness off the bench.

The plan seemed to be laid out perfectly, and we got off to a great start. We were 6-1 entering a tough seven-game Western swing in November, and proceeded to storm through the trip with six wins (including victories in San Antonio, Utah and Portland). Upon returning home we rattled off 10 consecutive wins to push our record to an incredible 23-2! I felt there were a couple of key wins in that stretch that helped us realize how good we could be. One was a victory over the Knicks on December 6 in which we rallied from an early 12-point deficit to win easily. The other was a triumph over the Magic a week later to avenge an early season loss in Orlando. That win was quite convincing, and seemed to exorcise the demons of the '95 playoffs.

So as we continued to play and win, we became more and more of a team. Roles were defined and teamwork developed, and our confidence soared. The 70-win question (which had first popped up in training camp) was now one we faced every single day. Publicly we downplayed it, but privately we not only wanted it, we expected it. After thumping the Knicks in Madison Square Garden to push our record to 35-3, Scottie Pippen said to me, "Seventy? Hell, I think we can win 75!" I didn't doubt him.

Meanwhile, Michael had clearly re-established himself as the best player in the game. Not only was he leading the league in scoring (and shooting over 50 percent), he was also taking over games on his own at will. He was good as ever, and he knew it. It showed in his eyes. His greatness was equaled only by his confidence.

Dennis, meanwhile, not only was the best rebounder in the league, but he had become arguably the most popular Bull in Chicago. The fans loved his hard work, his flamboyance, and most of all his habit of throwing his jersey into the stands after every home win. Signs were popping up all over the United Center begging Dennis for his uniform. My favorites were one that said simply, "Dennis — give me your damn jersey!" and another that said, "Dennis, my grandparents recently met you and found you to be a lovely young fellow — may I please have your jersey?"

Not only was he popular with the fans, he had also become quite a favorite of his teammates. It was hard not to like someone who rebounded and defended the way he did. But on top of that, the guys liked him. He was very quiet and reserved and honest, and genuinely nice to people; especially kids. My three-year-old son Nicholas immediately adopted Dennis as his favorite Bull after seeing his green hair, and Dennis always made a point of high-fiving the little boy whenever he saw him in the locker room.

As the season progressed, the team became more and more popular — in the United States and worldwide. The star power of Michael, Scottie and Dennis, along with the eclectic leadership style of Phil Jackson, had created a phenomenon at which the rest of us could only marvel. The team revelled in its popularity and the attention it received, but also began to feel some pressure. The questions suddenly went from "Can you win 70?" to "are you the greatest team ever?" The media coverage went from the *Chicago Tribune* and NBC Sports to "Dateline" and "Prime Time." We were being compared to the Beatles. All this and we hadn't won a thing yet — a division title, a playoff game, homecourt advantage — nothing. Still, our confidence was so high and our leadership so strong and unwavering that we never let down. We were prepared and focused every single night, and nothing bothered us. We just kept winning and winning, rolling toward the 70-win mark. We were so used to winning that on the rare occasion that we faltered and lost a game it was a shock. With an 82-game season in the NBA, losing (for most teams) becomes a way of life. For us it was stunning and motivating. We seemed to follow every defeat with a 10-game winning streak. We simply expected to win every night. Only we were mature enough to know that it wouldn't happen on its own.

When we finally did win our 70th game (in Milwaukee on April 16), we were excited but not jubilant. We had our eyes on the playoffs and, most importantly, winning the championship. And though the pressure was on us to win it all or face the label of being "chokers," we weren't fazed. In fact, we looked forward to the challenge. Ron and Scottie presented the team with T-shirts that read "72-10 — Don't mean a thing without the ring."

Miami was our first-round opponent and presented quite a challenge. Despite their Number Eight seed, the Heat was probably the third or fourth best team in the conference heading into the playoffs. Injuries had hurt their record early in the year but after a series of trades and some late-season momentum, they were confident. Game 1 was close at the half and our fans were a little nervous, but Ron Harper led a second half defensive surge that buried the Heat. We won going away, and followed that up with a blowout in Game 2. Miami was wary of our efforts, and it showed in Game 3. We stormed out of the blocks and played one of our best games of the year, sweeping the series 3-0.

That set up a matchup with our old friends the Knicks, a team the Bulls had faced in the playoffs four out of the previous five seasons. New York was a team that had defended us very well over the years and also had handed us our worst defeat of the season, a 32-point thrashing on March 10. We were confident, but respectful of their defensive efforts. We knew they'd play us well, and they did. We won the series in five tough games, including our first loss of the playoffs (in Game 3 in New York). The key to the series was

Game 4, in which Bill Wennington scored four points in the final minute to close out a come-from-behind win.

The 4-1 series win brought us to the series we had been waiting for all year — Orlando. They had stormed through the first two rounds of the playoffs, and the stage was set for a hyped battle between the two media darlings of the NBA — the Bulls and the Magic. Our team had been built to beat Orlando, constructed with personnel matchups in mind. The Magic was intent on a return trip to the Finals, where they had been humiliated by Houston the year before. NBC was reporting it as the "Series of the Century." Fortunately for us (and unfortunately for NBC), the series was anticlimactic. After a 38-point blowout in Game 1, we staged a huge comeback in Game 2 to go up 2-0. At that point the Magic players started dropping like flies. Injuries to Horace Grant, Brian Shaw, Nick Anderson and Jon Koncak left the team depleted, and we polished them off handily for a 4-0 sweep.

Just as in Milwaukee following our 70th win, the locker room celebration was excited yet subdued. We knew that despite gaining revenge over the Magic for last season's playoff loss, our final goal was still ahead — the championship.

While we were sweeping the Magic, Seattle and Utah were staging an epic battle in the West. The Sonics finally prevailed in seven games, by which time we had waited nine days between games. The anticipation was killing me, and the long layoff was physically trying as well. No matter how hard we practiced, there was no way to simulate the action of a real game — the adrenaline, the crowd, the tension. So we were somewhat concerned going into Game 1. We weren't sure how we'd respond. Of course Seattle was coming off a tiring seven-game series, so the question of the day was "Who will suffer — Chicago from inactivity or Seattle from fatigue?" Fortunately, it turned out to be the latter. We were a bit rusty but played decently, while Seattle played like a team that had celebrated too much after dispatching Utah. They seemed lifeless, and

for a team that relies on its trapping, gambling defense, that spelled doom. We won going away, 107-90.

Game 2 was much more difficult, and downright ugly. We won 92-88 in a terribly played game. Still, we were happy because we were headed to Seattle knowing we could play much better, and up 2-0 to boot. We felt we were due to play well in Game 3 and we did. In one of our best performances of the year we rocked the Sonics right from the opening tip and led by 24 at the half. Despite cutting the lead to 12, the Sonics could get no closer in the second half and we won going away.

It was at this point that the hype started. With a 3-0 lead a sweep seemed inevitable and the media changed its focus from us winning the series to our impending place in history. NBC lamented its bad luck, facing consecutive sweeps in the Finals (Houston the year before, now Chicago). The NBA staged a rehearsal of the championship celebration on the floor of Key Arena before Game 4 even started. Clearly everyone had forgotten how good Seattle was. They had won 64 games in the regular season (the 10th best record in league history). They were talented and athletic, yet their Finals inexperience had left them somewhat unsure of themselves in the first three games. Everyone, maybe even some of us, assumed the series was over.

Then they caught fire. They found their shooting strokes in Game 4, and their active defense combined with the loudest crowd I've ever heard made things awfully tough on us. They routed us in Game 4 and followed that up with a tough win in Game 5. All of a sudden it was a series again. We headed home up 3-2.

Again the media and fans changed the focus. We were no longer being considered for "best team ever" honors. Instead we were being labeled as chokers. We had played poorly in consecutive games in Seattle and it was now possible we could become the first team ever to lose a series after being up 3-0. When our plane landed at O'Hare upon returning from Seattle, Phil called us together for a meeting at the front of the plane. He went over strategic adjustments we would make and calmly explained the plan for Game 6. His message was clear: No need to get worked up — we're up 3-2 and playing at home; we're in great shape. Play hard and we'll win. It was at that point that I started to think about "the journey" that Phil had talked about before Game 2. This journey really had been a reward for the entire team. We had enjoyed a fabulous year and all we needed was one more win to put the perfect ending onto the season. Still, to lose two games and the series, in my mind, would spoil the journey. I have fond memories of the 1988 University of Arizona team (of which Jud Buechler and I were members) that went 35-3 and went to the NCAA Final Four. However, losing in the semi-finals to Oklahoma put a damper on that season that still bothers me today. We didn't complete the journey.

But the more I thought about the situation, the better I felt. We were up 3-2 with two shots at the championship at home in the United Center. On top of that, I thought about the strength of our team; the unwavering leadership of Phil; the imposing will of Michael; the talent and charisma of Scottie and Dennis; the unity that had developed between the entire team. We had travelled an amazing journey, and the journey had provided a rich reward. But it also had provided strength. We had travelled and fought and bonded together, and we had developed an amazing sense of unity and fortitude. There was no way we were going to lose. We were too strong.

The following day we beat Seattle in Game 6, 87-75, to win the NBA Championship. I'll never forget the feeling of utter joy and emotion as the clock ticked down. I jumped into Jud's arms as the buzzer sounded and bedlam ensued. The crowd was going crazy, Queen's "We Are the Champions" was blaring out of the United Center speakers, and the team converged at center court in a state of complete elation. After an unforgettable celebration amid 25,000 fans, we headed to the locker room to continue our fun. We poured champagne on each other, smoked victory cigars

and enjoyed one of the most emotional, gratifying moments of our lives. The journey was complete.

Yet now, as I reflect, my thoughts go well beyond the postgame party. I think about the efforts of the entire team and coaching staff throughout the season. I think about the shock of the rare defeats we were dealt, and the frenzied practices that followed. I think about hotels and restaurants, meals shared with teammates; long plane flights and bus trips; extra shooting every day after practice; lifting weights and stretching and icing to keep the legs strong through the season; sharing the agony of a bad game with my wife Margot late into a sleepless night; returning home after a long road trip to find my kids waiting for me. I realize that Phil was absolutely right. The journey is the reward.

Steve Kerr

June 17, 1996

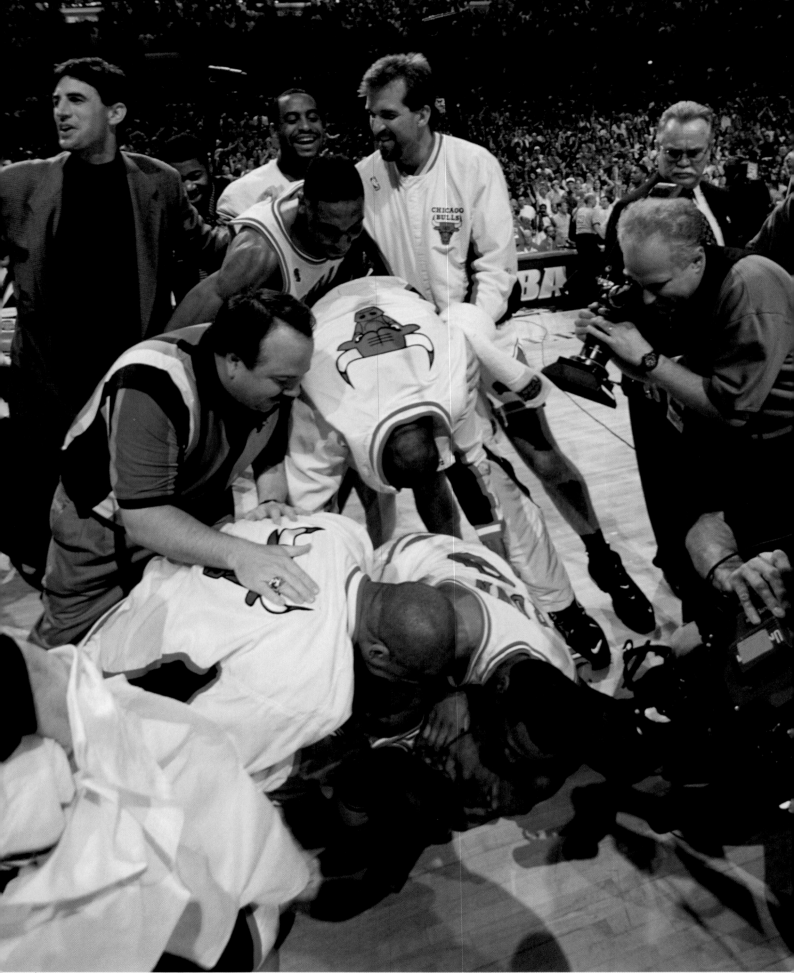

As his teammates converge on center court, MJ collapses
on the ball to start the post-championship festivities.

Final Series

Call Them World Champs— Bulls Come Home To Sink Seattle And Rewrite The Record Book

NBA Finals:
Seattle Supersonics
(4–2)

Game 1 in Chicago (W): 107–90
Game 2 in Chicago (W): 92–88
Game 3 at Seattle (W): 108–86
Game 4 at Seattle (L): 86–107
Game 5 at Seattle (L): 78–89
Game 6 in Chicago (W): 87–75

Was Dennis Rodman pushed by Frank Brickowski — or did he flop? That was the big question during the Seattle series. The answer depended on whom you asked — the referees or the Seattle Sonics.

Michael Jordan, Scottie Pippen and defensive sparkplug Randy Brown plan some strategy during game three. Brown, John Salley, Bill Wennington, Jud Buechler and Steve Kerr were among the reserves who helped win the "battle of the benches" against Seattle.

Scottie Pippen backs in against Gary Payton. Payton, the NBA's Defensive Player of the Year, had his hands full against the Bulls' relentless offense throughout the series.

Luc Longley turned into a dominating center against Seattle. He scored a playoff high of 19 points in the third game, and was a prominent force in every game.

During the Orlando series, Toni Kukoc drives through most of the Magic to score a crucial basket. Toni had a relatively quiet final series, but the game six clincher against the Sonics brought out the best in him and his teammates.

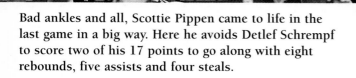

Bad ankles and all, Scottie Pippen came to life in the last game in a big way. Here he avoids Detlef Schrempf to score two of his 17 points to go along with eight rebounds, five assists and four steals.

MJ puts up a classic slam dunk during a
critical stage of the decisive game six.

MVP Michael Jordan savors a fourth championship moment.

In the first game of the Seattle finals, Toni Kukoc
showed why he won the NBA Sixth Man Award.
Coming off the bench, Toni scored 18 points, including
10 in a row during the critical third period.

SEATTLE (90)

	min	fg m–a	ft m–a	rb o–t	a	pf	tp
Kemp	41	9–14	14–16	5–8	2	6	32
Schrempf	35	3–8	6–6	3–8	3	4	13
Johnson	9	1–2	0–0	0–0	0	1	2
Hawkins	35	2–9	5–5	0–3	1	2	9
Payton	47	6–17	1–4	2–10	6	5	13
Perkins	37	5–11	1–1	4–5	2	3	14
McMillan	6	0–0	0–0	0–1	1	0	0
Askew	25	1–4	2–2	0–6	1	4	5
Brickowski	2	0–0	0–0	0–0	0	2	0
Wingate	2	0–0	2–2	0–0	0	2	2
Snow	1	0–0	0–0	0–0	0	0	0
Scheffler	DNP—coach's decision						
TOTALS	240	27–68	31–36	14–41	16	29	90

Percentages: FG–.397, FT–.861. **3-Point goals:** 5–16, .313 Perkins 3–5, Schrempf 1–2, Askew 1–3, Hawkins 0–3, Payton 0–3). **Team rebounds:**9. **Blocked shots:** 2 (Kemp, Johnson). **Turnovers:** 17 (Kemp 7, Payton 3, Perkins 3,Schrempf 2, Hawkins, Askew). **Steals:** 6 (Kemp 2, Schrempf, Johnson, Payton, Perkins).

CHICAGO (107)

	min	fg m–a	ft m–a	rb o–t	a	pf	tp
Pippen	44	5–15	8–9	5–7	3	3	21
Rodman	36	3–6	1–2	3–13	2	5	7
Longley	26	5–12	4–5	1–1	1	4	14
Harper	30	6–10	2–2	3–5	7	4	15
Jordan	41	9–18	9–10	0–7	2	4	28
Kerr	12	0–5	0–0	0–0	0	0	0
Kukoc	27	7–13	2–3	3–4	4	3	18
Brown	3	0–1	0–0	0–0	0	0	0
Wennington	10	2–2	0–0	2–3	0	0	4
Buechler	9	0–4	0–0	0–0	1	2	0
Edwards	DNP—coach's decision						
TOTALS	240	37–86	26–31	17–40	20	27	107

Pecentages: FG–.430, FT–.839. **3-Point goals:** 7–26, .269 (Pippen 3–8, Kukoc 2–5, Harper 1–3, Jordan 1–4, Kerr 0-3, Buechler 0–3). **Team rebounds:** 10. **Blocked shots:** 9 (Longley 4, Pippen 3, Harper, Jordan). **Turnovers:** 7 (Rodman 2, Jordan 2, Longley, Harper, Buechler). **Steals:** 9 (Pippen 3, Harper 2, Jordan 2, Rodman, Kukoc).

Seattle	18	30	29	13	–	90
Chicago	24	29	26	28	–	107

Technical Fouls: Chicago 2 (Rodman, 7:24 1st; Jordan, :26:3 3rd). Seattle 3 (Brickowski, 1:27 2nd; Payton, :26:3 3rd). **Flagrant fouls:** Seattle 1 (Brickowski, 1:27 second). **Ejections:** Seattle 1 (Brickowski, 1:27 second). **A:** 24,544. **T:** 2:26. **Officials:** Bennett Salavatore, Joe Crawford, Dan Crawford.

SEATTLE (88)

	min	fg m–a	ft m–a	rb o–t	a	pf	tp
Kemp	40	8–18	13–16	8–13	2	3	29
Schrempf	41	5–14	4–4	1–2	3	5	15
Johnson	8	1–4	0–0	6–7	1	5	2
Hawkins	39	6–11	3–5	0–2	0	5	16
Payton	45	6–15	0–0	0–5	3	5	13
Perkins	33	5–10	3–4	1–4	0	3	13
Askew	22	0–1	0–0	0–4	1	3	0
Brickowski	5	0–1	0–0	0–1	0	0	0
Wingate	5	0–0	0–0	0–1	0	1	0
Snow	2	0–1	0–0	0–0	0	0	0
McMillan	DNP—back injury						
Scheffler	DNP—coach's decision						
TOTALS	240	31–75	23–29	16–39	10	30	88

Percentages: FG–.413, FT–.793. **3-Point goals:** 3–15, .200 (Kemp 0–1, Schrempf 1—3, Hawkins 1–5, Payton 1–4, Perkins 0–1, Askew 0–1). **Team rebounds:** 7. **Blocked shots:** 4 (Kemp 4). **Turnovers:** 16 (Askew 4, Hawkins 3, Kemp 3, Perkins 3, Schrempf 2, Payton) **Steals:** 6 (Askew 2, Hawkins 2, Kemp, Payton).

CHICAGO (92)

	min	fg m–a	ft m–a	rb o–t	a	pf	tp
Pippen	38	8–16	5–8	3–7	2	3	21
Rodman	42	3–6	4–6	11–20	0	4	10
Longley	25	1–5	0–1	0–3	3	5	2
Harper	33	2–8	7–8	1–4	1	2	12
Jordan	43	9–22	10–16	2–6	8	3	29
Kukoc	24	4–12	1–2	3–5	5	2	11
Wennington	2	0–0	0–0	0–0	0	0	0
Kerr	13	1–6	1–1	0–0	0	2	3
Buechler	5	1–1	0–0	0–0	0	1	2
Salley	7	0–0	0–0	0–0	1	4	0
Brown	8	1–1	0–0	0–0	2	1	2
Edwards	DNP—coach's decision						
TOTALS	240	30–77	28–42	20–45	22	27	92

Percentages: FG–.390, FT–.667. **3-Point goals:** 4–21, .190 (Pippen 0–4, Jordan 1–2, Harper 1–4, Kukoc 2–7, Kerr 0–4). **Team rebounds:** 20. **Blocked shots:** 5 (Pippen 2, Longley 2, Kukoc). **Turnovers:** 15 (Rodman 4, Longley 3, Pippen 3, Brown 2, Jordan 2, Kukoc). **Steals:** 10 (Brown 2, Pippen 2, Beuchler 2, Longley 2, Jordan 2).

Seattle	27	18	20	23	–	88
Chicago	23	23	30	16	–	92

Technical fouls: Seattle 4 (Illegal Defense 4, 0:23 1st, 11:44 2nd, 5:44 2nd, 9:57 3rd). Chicago 3 (Illegal Defense 2, 9:18 2nd, 8:35 2nd; Assistant Coach Rodgers, 1:57 2nd). **Flagrant fouls:** Seattle 1 (Perkins, 6:31 3rd). **A:** 24,544. **T:** 2:48. **Officials:** Ed T Rush, Jess Kersey, Hue Hollins.

CHICAGO (108)

	min	fg m–a	ft m–a	rb o–t	a	pf	tp
Pippen	40	5–14	1–3	2–8	9	3	12
Rodman	31	1–3	3–6	3–10	2	5	5
Longley	28	8–13	3–4	2–3	2	5	19
Harper	1	0–0	0–0	0–0	0	0	0
Jordan	41	11–23	11–11	2–3	5	1	36
Kukoc	37	4–11	5–5	1–7	7	3	14
Wennington	15	3–4	0–0	0–0	1	4	6
Kerr	25	3–4	1–1	0–2	2	2	8
Buechler	8	1–2	0–2	0–0	0	1	2
Salley	4	0–0	0–0	0–0	0	2	0
Brown	10	2–2	1–2	0–0	0	3	6
Edwards	DNP—coach's decision						
TOTALS	240	38–76	25–34	10–33	28	29	108

Percentages: FG–.500, FT–.735. **3-Point goals:** 7–15, .467 (Pippen 1–4, Jordan 3–4, Kukoc 1–3, Kerr 1–2, Brown 1–1, Buechler 0–1). **Team rebounds:** 13. **Blocked shots:** 2 (Longley 2). **Turnovers:** 11 (Jordan 3, Rodman 2, Longley 2, Brown, Kerr). **Steals:** 9 (Pippen 3, Jordan 2, Buechler, Kerr, Kukoc, Rodman).

SEATTLE (86)

	min	fg m–a	ft m–a	rb o–t	a	pf	tp
Kemp	42	4–7	6–6	1–4	0	5	14
Schrempf	41	7–15	5–6	1–5	3	3	20
Johnson	3	0–0	0–0	0–0	0	0	0
Hawkins	40	2–6	7–7	0–1	2	4	12
Payton	45	7–15	5–6	2–7	9	2	19
Perkins	27	2–4	5–6	1–6	0	2	9
Askew	10	1–3	0–0	0–0	0	3	2
Brickowski	14	2–4	0–0	2–7	0	5	5
Wingate	12	2–5	0–0	0–0	0	3	5
Snow	3	0–1	0–0	0–2	0	2	0
Scheffler	3	0–0	0–0	0–0	0	0	0
McMillan	DNP—did not dress						
TOTALS	240	27–60	28–31	7–32	14	29	86

Percentages: FG–.450, FT–.903. **3-Point goals:** 4–16, .250 (Schrempf 1–5, Hawkins 1–3, Payton 0–3, Perkins 0–1, Askew 0–1, Brickowski 1–2, Wingate 1–1). **Team rebounds:** 5. **Blocked shots:** 4 (Kemp 4). **Turnovers:** 21 (Kemp 5, Askew 3, Schrempf 3, Payton 3, Brickowski 2, Hawkins 2, Perkins, Wingate) **Steals:** 3 (Payton 2, Hawkins).

Chicago	34	28	13	33	–	108
Seattle	16	22	23	25	–	86

Technical fouls: Seattle 2 (Payton, 11:22 4th; Schrempf, 2:43 4th). Chicago 1 (Rodman, 9:56 2nd). **Flagrant fouls:** Seattle 1 (Brickowski (ejected), 5:46 4th). **A:** 17,072. **T:** 2:31. **Officials:** Hugh Evans, Dick Bavetta, Steve Javie.

CHICAGO (86)

	min	fg m–a	ft m–a	rb o–t	a	pf	tp
Pippen	40	4–17	0–0	3–11	8	5	9
Rodman	41	4–6	0–0	8–14	4	5	8
Longley	25	5–8	2–2	1–3	3	5	12
Harper	13	1–3	0–0	0–1	0	1	2
Jordan	41	6–19	11–13	1–3	2	3	23
Kerr	22	1–6	2–2	1–1	1	0	5
Kukoc	30	6–11	0–0	0–1	1	3	14
Brown	13	3–5	1–2	1–2	2	1	9
Wennington	7	2–4	0–0	0–0	0	1	4
Buechler	7	0–1	0–0	0–0	0	0	0
Salley	1	0–0	0–0	0–0	1	0	0
Edwards	DNP—coach's decision						
TOTALS	240	32–80	16–19	15–36	22	24	86

Percentages: FG–.400, FT–.842. **3-Point goals:** 6–24, .250 (Pippen 1–8, Harper 0–1, Jordan 0–2, Kukoc 2–5, Kerr 1–4, Buechler 0–1, Brown 2–3). **Team rebounds:** 10. **Blocked shots:** 3 (Pippen 2, Longley). **Turnovers:** 18 (Kukoc 6, Jordan 4, Pippen 3, Buechler, Kerr, Longley, Rodman). **Steals:** 5 (Brown, Buechler, Jordan, Kukoc, Pippen).

SEATTLE (107)

	min	fg m–a	ft m–a	rb o–t	a	pf	tp
Kemp	33	12–17	1–1	3–11	3	4	25
Schrempf	42	6–13	1–2	2–5	3	1	14
Hawkins	37	6–9	4–4	3–6	2	3	18
Payton	44	7–15	4–6	0–3	11	4	21
Perkins	33	7–13	2–2	0–3	3	2	17
McMillan	14	2–3	2–2	0–3	3	2	8
Brickowski	16	0–0	0–0	0–2	0	5	0
Wingate	17	1–2	2–2	0–0	0	3	4
Snow	1	0–0	0–0	0–0	0	0	0
Scheffler	3	0–1	0–0	1–2	0	0	0
Johnson	DNP—coach's decision						
Askew	DNP—coach's decision						
TOTALS	240	41–73	16–19	9–35	25	24	107

Percentages: FG–.562, FT–.842. **3-Point goals:** 9–17, .529 (Schrempf 1–2, Hawkins 2–3, Payton 3–6, Perkins 1–3, McMillan 2–3). **Team rebounds:** 5. **Blocked shots:** 1 (Kemp). **Turnovers:** 15 (Brickowski 2, Schrempf 2, Payton 2, Perkins 2, Hawkins, Kemp, McMillan, Snow, Wingate). **Steals:** 7 (Kemp 2, Payton 2, Brickowski, Schrempf, Hawkins).

Chicago	21	11	31	23	–	86
Seattle	25	28	31	23	–	107

Technical fouls: Chicago 2 (Rodman, 7:28 1st; Jordan, 5:36 2nd). Seattle 3 (Brickowski, 9:14 3rd; Schrempf, 8:31 3rd; Wingate, 1:38 3rd). **Flagrant fouls:** Chicago 1 (Jordan, 0:56 3rd). **A:** 17,072. **T:** 2:23. **Officials:** Mike Mathis, Joe Crawford, Bill Oaks.

CHICAGO (78)

	min	fg m–a	ft m–a	rb o–t	a	pf	tp
Pippen	44	5–20	3–4	5–8	5	4	14
Rodman	37	2–5	2–2	5–12	2	5	6
Longley	34	3–3	5–7	0–5	4	4	11
Harper	1	0–0	0–0	0–0	0	0	0
Jordan	43	11–24	4–5	2–4	1	3	26
Kerr	24	2–8	2–3	0–1	2	3	7
Kukoc	37	5–13	0–0	2–9	3	3	11
Brown	10	0–2	0–0	0–0	1	3	0
Wennington	6	1–2	1–2	0–0	0	2	3
Buechler	3	0–1	0–0	0–0	0	0	0
Salley	1	0–1	0–0	1–1	0	0	0
Edwards	DNP—coach's decision						
TOTALS	**240**	**29–77**	**17–23**	**15–40**	**18**	**27**	**78**

Percentages: FG–.377, FT–.739. **3-Point goals:** 3–26, .115 (Kukoc 1–5, Kerr 1–7, Pippen 1–8, Buechler 0–1, Brown 0–1, Jordan 0–4). **Team rebounds:** 11. **Blocked shots:** 2 (Pippen, Longley). **Turnovers:** 13 (Pippen 2, Rodman 2, Longley 2, Jordan 2, Kukoc 2, Wennington 2, Kerr). **Steals:** 3 (Pippen, Jordan, Kukoc).

SEATTLE (75)

	min	fg m–a	ft m–a	rb o–t	a	pf	tp
Kemp	40	8–17	2–2	6–14	3	6	18
Schrempf	40	9–17	3–4	1–5	2	3	23
Hawkins	41	2–6	0–0	1–4	0	4	4
Payton	47	7–10	2–2	0–4	7	3	19
Perkins	32	3–14	1–2	3–6	5	0	7
McMillan	10	0–3	0–0	0–1	0	0	0
Brickowski	14	0–3	0–0	0–0	1	1	0
Wingate	9	2–2	0–0	1–1	0	3	4
Askew	5	0–1	0–0	0–0	0	0	0
Snow	1	0–0	0–0	0–0	1	0	0
Scheffler	1	0–0	0–0	0–0	0	0	0
Johnson	DNP—coach's decision						
TOTALS	**240**	**31–73**	**8–10**	**12–35**	**19**	**20**	**75**

Percentages: FG–.425, FT–.800. **3-Point goals:** 5–24, .208 (Payton 3–5, Schrempf 2–5, McMillan 0–1, Brickowski 0–2, Hawkins 0–4, Perkins 0–7). **Team rebounds:** 8. **Blocked shots:** 3 (Kemp 2, Brickowski). **Turnovers:** 20 (Schrempf 5, Payton 5, Kemp 4, Hawkins 3, Perkins, McMillan, Wingate). **Steals:** 10 (Kemp 3, Hawkins 2, Payton 2, Schrempf, Perkins, McMillan).

SEATTLE (89)

	min	fg m–a	ft m–a	rb o–t	a	pf	tp
Kemp	46	8–16	6–8	3–10	3	4	22
Schrempf	39	5–12	2–2	1–5	1	2	13
Hawkins	38	7–14	5–5	3–5	1	3	21
Payton	46	7–18	7–8	2–9	6	3	23
Perkins	28	1–6	5–6	0–4	2	3	7
McMillan	21	1–1	0–0	0–6	2	4	3
Brickowski	17	0–1	0–0	0–2	2	3	0
Wingate	3	0–1	0–0	0–0	0	1	0
Snow	1	0–0	0–0	0–0	0	0	0
Scheffler	1	0–0	0–0	0–0	0	0	0
Askew	DNP—coach's decision						
Johnson	DNP—coach's decision						
TOTALS	**240**	**29–69**	**25–29**	**9–41**	**17**	**23**	**89**

Percentages: FG–.420, FT–.862. **3-Point goals:** 6–14, .429 (Schrempf 1–1, Hawkins 2–4, Payton 2–6, McMillan 1–1, Brickowski 0–1, Wingate 0–1). **Team rebounds:** 6. **Blocked shots:** 2 (Schrempf, Hawkins). **Turnovers:** 11 (Kemp 4, Schrempf 2, Hawkins 2, Payton, McMillan). **Steals:** 4 (Hawkins, Payton, Perkins, McMillan).

Chicago	18	24	18	18	–	78
Seattle	18	25	19	27	–	89

Technical fouls: Chicago 2 (Illegal defense, 11:01 2nd; Delay, 5:55 3rd). Seattle 1 (McMillan, 8:13 2nd). **Flagrant fouls:** None. **A:** 17,072. **T:** 2:36. **Officials:** Ed T Rush, Jess Kersey, Hue Hollins.

CHICAGO (87)

	min	fg m–a	ft m–a	rb o–t	a	pf	tp
Pippen	42	7–17	0–0	2–8	5	4	17
Rodman	38	4–9	1–3	11–19	5	4	9
Longley	32	5–6	2–3	4–8	0	0	12
Harper	38	3–11	2–2	0–3	2	1	10
Jordan	43	5–19	11–12	3–9	7	3	22
Kerr	17	3–4	0–0	1–1	0	1	7
Kukoc	22	4–11	0–0	3–3	1	0	10
Brown	5	0–1	0–0	0–0	0	2	0
Wennington	2	0–0	0–0	0–0	0	0	0
Buechler	1	0–0	0–0	0–0	0	0	0
Salley	DNP—coach's decision						
Edwards	DNP—coach's decision						
TOTALS	**240**	**31–78**	**16–20**	**24–51**	**20**	**15**	**87**

Percentages: FG–.397, FT–.800. **3-Point goals:** 9–25, .360 (Pippen 3–7, Harper 2–5, Kukoc 2–7, Kerr 1–2, Jordan 1–3, Brown 0–1). **Team rebounds:** 1. **Blocked shots:** 4 (Rodman, Longley, Harper, Kukoc). **Turnovers:** 19 (Longley 6, Jordan 5, Pippen 3, Harper 2, Kukoc 2, Kerr). **Steals:** 14 (Pippen 4, Rodman 3, Harper 2, Jordan 2, Longley, Kukoc, Brown).

Seattle	18	20	20	17	–	75
Chicago	24	21	22	20	–	87

Technical fouls: Seattle 1 (Payton, 4:39 2nd). Chicago 1 (Pippen, 4:39 2nd). **Flagrant fouls:** None. **A:** 24,544. **T:** 2:18. **Officials:** Hugh Evans, Dick Bavetta, Steve Javie.

A bit o' the green peeks out from beneath his towel.

Rodmania strikes these wannabes.

Snow white was a change of pace for the Worm.

Rodman's Dye Jobs

As Colorful As He Wants To Be

During the early part of the regular season. Dennis sported yellow with a red swirl.

What would the NBA be without Dennis Rodman? After being traded from the San Antonio Spurs in the preseason for Will Perdue (thank you, Spurs), the well-traveled Worm made an immediate impact on his new team. Not knowing what to expect, Phil Jackson welcomed Rodman to the Bulls with the hope his coaching methods would jump-start Dennis' career and solve Chicago's need for a rebounder and force inside. And what a force #91 would prove to be.

The rollicking season featured a lot of ejections, including the head-butt heard around the world, even more technical fouls, a few rim-rocking, crowd-shocking three pointers, emotional outbursts, controversial quotes, crazy outfits, a best-selling book—and rebounds, rebounds, and more rebounds. In the end, hard work and heart paid off. The Worm captured his fifth consecutive NBA rebounding title with a 14.9 boards per game average and first team all-defense honors. And, on balance, he behaved.

Overcoming years of booing as the baddest of the Detroit "Bad Boys," Dennis won the Chicago fans over in part by throwing his jersey to a lucky fan after each United Center victory. After having gone through more hair colors than a box of crayons, a new Chicago legend was born in the city that adopted him with open arms.

...so was cotton candy...

Rustoleum was a popular Rodman "do" selection.

...and fire engine red.

Don't mess with Dennis.

Dennis had a special treat fo
the Miami Heat Series—red, orang
and yellow flames

Shirt in hand, a blonde Rodman
looks for the lucky fan who will
get the night's jersey after the
first Seattle Sonics game.

For the finals, the Rodman hairdo was full of color and symbols. Icons included an AIDS ribbon, a logo for the rock band Pearl Jam, a peace sign, and, apparently in tribute to Coach Jackson, Zen symbols and tribal art.

Magic Series

No Sweat: Bulls Sweep Magic In Four Games

Eastern Conference Finals:
Orlando Magic
(4–0)

Game 1 in Chicago (W): 121–83
Game 2 in Chicago (W): 93–88
Game 3 at Orlando (W): 86–67
Game 4 at Orlando (W): 106–101

Michael squeezes through a Shaquille O'Neal pick to stay on Penny Hardaway's trail.

Toni Kukoc turns the corner on Penny as he drives toward the hoop.

Pippen jams home a first game fastbreak as Anfernee Hardaway and Horace Grant play catch-up.

Just what the league has feared...another weapon to add to the Bulls offensive arsenal. Dennis Rodman startled the Magic with his clutch baskets throughout the series.

e heart of the Magic,
fernee (Penny) Hardaway
es in for a lay-up on
chael Jordan.

Scottie Pippen glides by Shaq and Dennis Scott
for a reverse lay-up during game one.
© 1996 NATHANIEL S. BUTLER / NBA PHOTOS

© 1996 NATHANIEL S. BUTLER / NBA PHOTOS
Where can Hardaway go? MJ, Rodman, and Harp cut off
all access to the hole.

Toni Kukoc pops a wide-open jumper as Nick Anderson scrambles to defend.

Dennis rejects a Hardaway stuff.
All through the four games, the Bulls team
defense stopped just about everything
the Magic threw at them.

The Worm springs for a rebound as only he can.

ORLANDO (83)

	min	fg m–a	ft m–a	rb o–t	a	pf	tp
Grant	28	0–1	0–0	0–1	0	1	0
Scott	26	0–3	0–0	0–2	0	2	0
O'Neal	40	13–21	1–7	0–6	6	2	27
Anderson	30	0–7	2–6	1–5	2	1	2
Hardaway	40	15–21	4–7	1–3	3	1	38
Shaw	28	2–4	0–0	0–2	3	1	5
Koncak	4	0–1	0–0	1–1	0	1	0
Bowie	19	2–7	0–0	1–3	2	2	4
Royal	14	2–2	0–2	1–2	1	0	4
Thompson	5	1–2	0–0	0–1	0	1	2
Wolf	3	0–4	1–2	0–1	0	0	1
Bonner	3	0–0	0–0	1–1	0	0	0
TOTALS	240	35–73	8–24	6–28	17	12	83

Percentages: FG–.479, FT–.333. **3-Point goals:** 5–16, .313 (Scott 0–2, Anderson 0–4, Hardaway 4–6, Shaw 1–2, Wolf 0–2). **Team rebounds:** 7. **Blocked shots:** 1 (Bowie). **Turnovers:** 16 (Hardaway 4, O'Neal 3, Shaw 2, Anderson, Grant, Koncak, Royal, Scott, Thompson, Wolf). **Steals:** 8 (Hardaway 3, O'Neal 2, Anderson, Bowie, Koncak).

ORLANDO (88)

	min	fg m–a	ft m–a	rb o–t	a	pf	tp
Koncak	22	1–2	1–2	2–5	1	4	3
Scott	42	4–9	4–5	1–3	3	1	13
O'Neal	44	16–22	4–8	7–16	4	2	36
Anderson	42	3–11	2–3	1–4	0	4	9
Hardaway	44	6–15	5–7	0–2	3	6	18
Shaw	28	3–9	0–0	3–6	6	4	7
Bowie	11	1–1	0–0	0–1	0	2	2
Royal	7	0–2	0–0	0–0	0	2	0
Thompson	DNP—coach's decision						
Grant	DNP—twisted left elbow						
Wolf	DNP—coach's decision						
Bonner	DNP—coach's decision						
TOTALS	240	34–71	16–25	14–37	17	25	88

Percentages: FG–.479, FT–.640. **3-Point goals:** 4–19, .211 (Scott 1–4, Anderson 1–7, Hardaway 1–5, Shaw 1–3). **Team rebounds:** 10. **Blocked shots:** 2 (Koncak, O'Neal). **Turnovers:** 18 (O'Neal 6, Anderson 4, Hardaway 3, Shaw 2, Koncak, Scott). **Steals:** 4 (Anderson, O'Neal, Scott, Shaw).

CHICAGO (121)

	min	fg m–a	ft m–a	rb o–t	a	pf	tp
Pippen	35	7–20	3–4	3–8	4	2	18
Rodman	32	6–10	1–1	7–21	1	4	13
Longley	13	7–9	0–0	2–3	1	4	14
Harper	30	4–7	0–0	4–7	6	1	8
Jordan	37	9–17	2–3	2–7	4	3	21
Kukoc	32	5–10	2–2	0–6	10	0	12
Wennington	15	3–7	0–0	0–2	0	2	6
Brown	8	1–2	0–0	0–1	1	1	2
Kerr	17	5–7	0–0	0–4	6	2	14
Buechler	14	2–3	0–0	1–1	2	0	5
Salley	7	4–4	0–2	1–2	2	3	8
Edwards	DNP—coach's decision						
TOTALS	240	53–96	8–12	20–62	37	22	121

Percentages: FG–.552, FT–.667. **3-Point goals:** 7–19, .368 (Pippen 1–7, Harper 0–1, Jordan 1–2, Kukoc 0–3, Kerr 4–5, Buechler 1–1). **Team rebounds:** 4. **Blocked shots:** 2 (Rodman, Salley). **Turnovers:** 13 (Jordan 3, Rodman 3, Harper 2, Kukoc 2, Brown, Pippen, Salley). **Steals:** 12 (Kerr 3, Harper 2, Jordan 2, Kukoc 2, Longley 2, Pippen).

Orlando	19	26	14	24	–	83	
Chicago	32	23	26	40	–	121	

Technical fouls: Orlando 1 (Hardaway, 6:04 3rd). **Flagrant fouls:** None. **A:** 24,411. **T:** 2:19.
Officials: Ron Garretson, Bennett Salvatore, Hugh Evans.

CHICAGO (93)

	min	fg m–a	ft m–a	rb o–t	a	pf	tp
Pippen	46	7–19	2–6	6–10	9	2	17
Rodman	35	6–8	3–6	6–12	1	2	15
Longley	24	0–5	0–0	2–8	1	5	0
Harper	32	3–9	1–2	1–3	2	3	8
Jordan	43	9–21	15–16	1–5	6	2	35
Kukoc	28	1–7	4–4	1–2	5	5	6
Wennington	10	1–2	0–0	0–2	0	1	2
Kerr	15	1–2	1–2	1–2	1	0	3
Buechler	6	2–2	0–0	0–0	2	0	5
Brown	1	0–0	0–0	0–0	0	1	2
Salley	DNP—coach's decision						
Edwards	DNP—coach's decision						
TOTALS	240	30–75	28–38	18–44	27	21	93

Percentages: FG–.400, FT–.737. **3-Point goals:** 5–19, .263 (Pippen 1–7, Harper 1–4, Jordan 2–4, Kukoc 0–2, Kerr 0–1, Buechler 1–1). **Team rebounds:** 10. **Blocked shots:** 2 (Longley, Jordan). **Turnovers:** 9 (Jordan 2, Kukoc 2, Pippen 2, Harper). **Steals:** 12 (Jordan 4, Pippen 3, Harper 2, Rodman 2, Kukoc).

Orlando	23	30	16	19	–	88	
Chicago	20	18	29	26	–	93	

Technical fouls: Orlando 1 (O'Neal, 4:21 2nd). Chicago 4 (Kukoc, 10:51 2nd; Illegal Defense 3, 3:21 2nd, 11:04 3rd, 6:34 4th). **Flagrant fouls:** None. **A:** 24,395. **T:** 2:29.
Officials: Bill Oakes, Joe Crawford, Ed Middleton.

CHICAGO (86)

	min	fg m–a	ft m–a	rb o–t	a	pf	tp
Pippen	41	11–14	2–4	2–6	7	1	27
Rodman	40	2–6	5–8	6–16	0	4	9
Longley	30	3–11	4–5	1–5	1	5	10
Harper	26	3–9	1–2	2–4	0	2	8
Jordan	39	5–14	6–11	3–7	4	1	17
Kukoc	20	1–5	0–0	1–5	1	1	3
Wennington	8	2–3	0–0	0–1	0	4	4
Kerr	15	3–6	0–1	0–0	2	0	8
Buechler	12	0–1	0–0	0–0	0	1	0
Salley	5	0–0	0–0	0–1	0	2	0
Brown	4	0–0	0–0	0–0	0	2	0
Edwards	DNP—coach's decision						
TOTALS	**240**	**30–69**	**18–31**	**15–45**	**15**	**23**	**86**

Percentages: FG–.435, FT–.581. **3-Point goals:** 8–16, .500 (Pippen 3–4, Jordan 1–1, Harper 1–3, Kukoc 1–2, Kerr 2–5, Buechler 0–1). **Team rebounds:** 19. **Blocked shots:** 7 (Harper 2, Longley 2, Pippen, Rodman, Jordan). **Turnovers:** 19 (Pippen 4, Rodman 4, Kukoc 3, Jordan 2, Kerr 2, Longley 2, Buechler). **Steals:** 9 (Harper 2, Jordan 2, Pippen 2, Buechler, Kerr, Kukoc).

ORLANDO (67)

	min	fg m–a	ft m–a	rb o–t	a	pf	tp
Koncak	20	0–0	1–2	0–0	0	4	1
Scott	37	1–9	4–6	1–4	0	5	7
O'Neal	45	8–19	1–9	6–12	3	4	17
Anderson	40	6–11	0–2	2–7	0	2	14
Hardaway	46	8–24	0–0	2–7	3	1	18
Bowie	9	0–2	0–0	0–0	2	1	0
Royal	15	2–3	2–3	1–1	0	0	6
Thompson	12	1–7	2–2	2–1	2	1	4
Wolf	10	0–1	0–0	0–1	1	3	0
Bonner	6	0–1	0–0	1–1	0	2	0
Grant	DNP—twisted left elbow						
Shaw	DNP—neck spasms						
TOTALS	**240**	**26–77**	**10–24**	**14–34**	**10**	**23**	**67**

Percentages: FG–.338, FT–.417. **3-Point goals:** 5–23, .217 (Scott 1–7, Anderson 2–4, Hardaway 2–9, Thompson 0–3). **Team rebounds:** 19. **Blocked shots:** 4 (O'Neal 2, Koncak, Royal). **Turnovers:** 16 (O'Neal 5, Anderson 3, Hardaway 3, Thompson 3, Wolf). **Steals:** 10 (Anderson 4, O'Neal 2, Scott 2, Hardaway, Koncak).

Chicago	23	25	15	23	—	86
Orlando	20	18	19	10	—	67

Technical fouls: Chicago 2 (Rodman, 2:05 1st; Asst. Coach T Winter, 1:31 2nd). Orlando 3 (Head Coach Hill, 0:13 1st; O'Neal, 10:30 2nd; Delay, 6:42 2nd). **Flagrant fouls:** Orlando 1 (Koncak, 8:40 1st). **A:** 17,248. **T:** 2:25. **Officials:** Ed F Rush, Ed T Rush, Steve Javie.

CHICAGO (106)

	min	fg m–a	ft m–a	rb o–t	a	pf	tp
Pippen	42	4–11	3–6	2–5	8	4	12
Rodman	41	2–6	5–8	7–14	2	3	9
Longley	22	3–6	0–0	2–5	1	6	6
Harper	26	4–8	3–5	0–2	2	2	12
Jordan	44	16–23	10–14	2–3	5	5	45
Kukoc	24	2–6	2–2	0–0	3	2	7
Wennington	2	0–2	0–0	0–0	1	0	0
Kerr	27	3–5	2–2	0–1	1	4	9
Buechler	7	2–2	0–0	0–0	0	1	6
Salley	1	0–1	0–0	1–1	0	0	0
Edwards	3	0–0	0–0	0–0	0	2	0
Brown	1	0–0	0–0	0–0	0	0	0
TOTALS	**240**	**36–70**	**25–37**	**14–31**	**23**	**29**	**106**

Percentages: FG–.514, FT–.676. **3-Point goals:** 9–22, .409 (Pippen 1–5, Jordan 3–4, Harper 1–3, Kukoc 1–5, Buechler 2–2, Kerr 1–3). **Team rebounds:** 13. **Blocked shots:** 4 (Rodman, Jordan, Harper, Kukoc). **Turnovers:** 17 (Longley 5, Jordan 4, Harper 2, Kukoc 2, Pippen 2, Rodman). **Steals:** 12 (Harper 3, Kerr 3, Pippen 2, Buechler, Jordan, Kukoc, Rodman).

ORLANDO (101)

	min	fg m–a	ft m–a	rb o–t	a	pf	tp
Scott	36	4–13	0–2	1–1	3	5	9
O'Neal	42	11–13	6–9	1–9	3	5	28
Hardaway	45	9–21	9–12	0–3	8	3	28
Koncak	19	1–1	0–0	1–2	1	4	2
Bowie	34	3–6	2–2	0–4	2	4	8
Royal	25	1–1	2–2	0–2	0	3	4
Thompson	27	7–10	2–3	2–3	3	4	17
Wolf	12	1–1	2–2	0–0	0	2	5
Bonner	DNP—coach's decision						
Grant	DNP—twisted left elbow						
Anderson	DNP—sprained right wrist						
Shaw	DNP—coach's decision						
TOTALS	**240**	**37–66**	**23–32**	**5–24**	**20**	**30**	**101**

Percentages: FG–.561, FT–.719. **3-Point goals:** 4–15, .267 (Scott 1–6, Hardaway 1–6, Thompson 1–2, Wolf 1–1). **Team rebounds:** 16. **Blocked shots:** 4 (O'Neal 3, Hardaway). **Turnovers:** 16 (Thompson 4, Bowie 3, Hardaway 3, O'Neal 3, Royal, Scott). **Steals:** 5 (Scott 2, Bowie, Koncak, O'Neal).

Chicago	23	24	28	31	—	106
Orlando	31	25	18	27	—	101

Technical fouls: Chicago 3 (Illegal Defense 2, 5:57 2nd; 7:26 4th; Rodman, 1:31 2nd). Orlando 2 (O'Neal, 1:31 2nd; 10:04 3rd). **Flagrant fouls:** None. **A:** 17,248. **T:** 2:40. **Officials:** Dick Bavetta, Hue Hollins, Dan Crawford.

Knicks Series

Physical Knicks Take Toll On Bulls—But It's Bulls In Five

Eastern Conference Semi-finals:
New York Knicks
(4–1)

Game 1 in Chicago (W): 91–84
Game 2 in Chicago (W): 91–80
Game 3 at New York (L): 99–102
Game 4 at New York (W): 94–91
Game 5 in Chicago (W): 94–81

You just knew it was going to be a war. The Knicks hammered, pushed and antagonized the Bulls during the five-game series. Here, Dennis Rodman posts up against Anthony Mason as they get set for a rebound.

Michael in his rare air flies by old friend Charles Oakley for a reverse.

Three-point specialist, Steve Kerr, brings the ball up court in the Garden. Kerr summed up the Bulls rivalry with New York by acknowledging there's "...a genuine hatred with the Knicks."

Harp attempts a
fifteen-footer over the
towering Pat Ewing
in game five.

DENIED! Pippen and Jordan let New York's John Starks
know he will not be driving the lane against the Bulls.
Playing on Stark's emotions, the Bulls frustrated the Knicks
guard throughout the series.

Taking on Patrick Ewing, Bill Wennington is one of the Bulls
who might not grab the headlines, but makes valuable contributions
off the bench. In game three, Bill brought Madison Square Garden
to a silent standstill after sinking the final second shot that sent
the game into overtime.

Despite a game five ejection, Dennis Rodman dominated the Knicks series with a total of 78 rebounds. Here, Dennis ponders a game four technical, perhaps wondering why the refs constantly pick on the Worm.

Luc drives through traffic in the first game against New York. Each Longley score is followed by a rousing "LUUUUUUUUUUUUUUU-UUUUC!!!" from United Center fans.

ook it. Michael's tongue is out as he blows by Willie Anderson. You know what's coming.

Game One

NEW YORK (84)

	min	fg m–a	ft m–a	rb o–t	a	pf	tp
Oakley	43	4–9	6–7	6–13	2	4	14
Mason	45	5–11	2–2	1–5	2	4	12
Ewing	43	9–23	3–5	3–16	1	3	21
Starks	39	0–9	4–4	2–2	2	4	4
Harper	40	8–17	1–2	0–0	5	2	19
Ward	8	2–5	0–0	0–0	1	0	4
Davis	15	3–4	0–0	0–3	0	2	8
Reid	7	1–1	0–0	0–1	1	2	2
Anderson	DNP—coach's decision						
Grandison	DNP—coach's decision						
Grant	DNP—coach's decision						
Williams	DNP—coach's decision						
TOTALS	240	32–79	16–20	12–40	14	21	84

Percentages: FG–.405, FT–.800. **3-Point goals:** 4–15, .267 (Starks 0–5, Harper 2–5, Ward 0–2, Davis 2–3). **Team rebounds:** 13. **Blocked shots:** None. **Turnovers:** 17 (Ewing 5, Davis 3, Mason 3, Oakley 3, Harper, Reid Starks). **Steals:** 4 (Harper 2, Ewing, Ward).

CHICAGO (91)

	min	fg m–a	ft m–a	rb o–t	a	pf	tp
Pippen	43	4–15	3–3	5–10	7	0	11
Rodman	33	0–3	3–4	3–12	2	4	3
Longley	35	4–10	0–0	5–8	2	5	8
Harper	30	2–7	0–0	2–7	3	3	4
Jordan	41	17–35	9–9	1–5	2	4	44
Kukoc	28	1–8	5–6	1–2	5	2	7
Kerr	15	3–6	0–0	0–1	0	0	8
Salley	2	0–0	0–0	0–0	0	0	0
Edwards	7	0–0	2–2	0–0	0	2	2
Brown	2	1–2	0–0	0–0	0	1	2
Wennington	4	1–1	0–0	1–3	0	2	2
Buechler	DNP—coach's decision						
TOTALS	240	33–87	22–24	18–48	21	23	91

Percentages: FG–.379, FT–.917. **3-Point goals:** 3-19, .158 (Pippen 0–4, Harper 0–2, Jordan 1–5, Kukoc 0–4, Kerr 2–4). **Team rebounds:** 6. **Blocked shots:** 4 (Longley 2, Pippen, Harper). **Turnovers:** 9 (Rodman 3, Kerr 2, Jordan, Longley, Pippen). **Steals:** 8 (Kukoc 2, Longley 2, Pippen 2, Harper, Rodman).

New York	17	30	22	15	–	84
Chicago	25	29	19	18	–	91

Technical fouls: New York 3 (Harper, 4:49 2nd; Mason 8:49 3rd; Oakley, 7:59 4th). Chicago 2 (Jordan, 4:49 2nd; Pippen, 7:59 4th). **Flagrant fouls:** None. **A:** 24,394. **T:** 2:24. **Officials:** Ed F Rush, Don Vaden, Joe Crawford.

Game Two

NEW YORK (80)

	min	fg m–a	ft m–a	rb o–t	a	pf	tp
Oakley	39	3–10	3–6	6–11	0	4	9
Mason	44	5–10	0–0	3–8	1	2	10
Ewing	39	9–19	5–9	1–10	1	2	23
Starks	32	2–5	8–8	0–3	4	4	12
Harper	40	4–13	0–0	0–1	5	4	11
Davis	19	0–4	1–2	0–0	2	3	1
Grant	8	2–5	0–0	2–3	0	0	6
Williams	9	1–2	0–0	0–0	0	0	2
Anderson	10	2–6	2–2	1–2	0	2	6
Grandison	DNP—coach's decision						
Reid	DNP—coach's decision						
Ward	DNP—flu						
TOTALS	240	28–74	19–27	13–38	13	21	80

Percentages: FG–.378, FT–.704. **3-Point goals:** 5–19, .263 (Oakley 0–1, Starks 0–1, Harper 3–8, Davis 0–4, Grant 2–3, Anderson 0–2). **Team rebounds:** 10. **Blocked shots:** 4 (Ewing 4). **Turnovers:** 20 (Harper 5, Ewing 4, Oakley 4, Mason 3, Starks 3, Grant). **Steals:** 8 (Starks 4, Anderson, Grant, Harper, Mason).

CHICAGO (91)

	min	fg m–a	ft m–a	rb o–t	a	pf	tp
Pippen	41	7–21	2–2	2–5	6	4	19
Rodman	31	3–4	0–0	5–19	1	4	6
Longley	25	3–6	0–0	4–9	0	5	6
Harper	33	5–13	3–4	4–9	3	4	15
Jordan	40	11–25	5–5	3–5	5	0	28
Kukoc	25	2–7	2–2	0–2	2	3	6
Kerr	19	2–5	0–0	0–0	1	1	5
Buechler	4	0–2	0–0	0–2	0	0	0
Edwards	5	1–2	0–0	0–2	0	2	2
Wennington	14	1–1	0–0	0–3	1	3	3
Salley	3	0–0	1–2	0–0	0	0	1
Brown	DNP—coach's decision						
TOTALS	240	35–86	14–17	18–54	19	26	91

Percentages: FG–.407, FT–.824. **3-Point goals:** 7–21, .333 (Pippen 3–7, Harper 2–3, Jordan 1–3, Kukoc 0–4, Kerr 1–2, Buechler 0–2). **Team rebounds:** 6. **Blocked shots:** 6 (Longley 3, Rodman 2, Pippen). **Turnovers:** 18 (Rodman 5, Longley 3, Buechler 2, Harper 2, Jordan 2, Pippen 2, Kerr). **Steals:** 9 (Pippen 4, Jordan 3, Kukoc, Wennington).

New York	19	22	8	21	–	80
Chicago	22	20	19	30	–	91

Technical fouls: New York 3 (Ewing, 6:46 lst; Harper, 4:46 4th; Starks, 3:41 4th). Chicago 2 (Assistant Coach Cleamons, 6:46 4th; Harper, 3:41 4th). **Flagrant fouls:** None. **A:** 24,328. **T:** 2:19. **Officials:** Bernie Fryer, Jack Nies, Jess Kersey.

Game Three

CHICAGO (99)

	min	fg m–a	ft m–a	rb o–t	a	pf	tp
Rodman	52	2–4	3–3	2–16	3	4	7
Pippen	49	10–29	0–0	4–8	6	4	24
Longley	26	3–7	0–0	0–1	1	5	6
Jordan	51	17–35	10–13	3–4	2	2	46
Harper	36	1–8	1–2	1–3	1	5	4
Wennington	15	2–4	0–0	2–3	0	3	4
Kerr	24	3–5	0–0	0–0	3	1	6
Buechler	7	0–0	2–2	0–1	0	2	2
Salley	4	0–0	0–0	0–0	0	2	0
Edwards	1	0–0	0–0	0–0	0	0	0
Brown	DNP—coach's decision						
Kukoc	DNP—sore lower back						
TOTALS	**265**	**38–92**	**16—20**	**12–36**	**16**	**28**	**99**

Percentages: FG–.413, FT–.800. **3-Point goals:** 7–21, .333 (Pippen 4–11, Jordan 2–5, Harper 1–4, Kerr 0–1). **Team rebounds:** 8. **Blocked shots:** 2 (Rodman, Harper). **Turnovers:** 14 (Jordan 4, Pippen 4, Rodman 3, Kerr, Wennington). **Steals:** 12 (Pippen 3, Rodman 3, Harper 2, Jordan 2, Kerr 2).

NEW YORK (102)

	min	fg m–a	ft m–a	rb o–t	a	pf	tp
Oakley	44	4–8	5–6	4–13	2	4	13
Mason	49	7–10	4–6	3–10	2	2	18
Ewing	45	8–15	6–8	2–13	3	2	22
Starks	43	11–18	3–5	0–4	6	5	30
Harper	39	1–11	1–1	0–1	2	2	3
Ward	20	5–6	2–4	1–3	2	1	12
Davis	7	0–1	0–0	0–1	0	1	0
Anderson	18	1–6	2–3	0–1	0	2	4
Grandison	DNP—coach's decision						
Grant	DNP—coach's decision						
Reid	DNP—coach's decision						
Williams	DNP—coach's decision						
TOTALS	**265**	**37–75**	**23–33**	**10–46**	**17**	**19**	**102**

Percentages: FG–.493, FT–.697. **3-Point goals:** 5–17, .294 (Oakley 0–1, Starks 5–8, Harper 0–5, Ward 0–1, Anderson 0–2). **Team rebounds:** 16. **Blocked shots:** 3 (Ewing 3). **Turnovers:** 21 (Oakley 7, Anderson 3, Mason 3, Starks 3, Harper 2, Ewing, Ward). **Steals:** 9 (Starks 3, Oakley 2, Anderson, Harper, Mason, Ward).

Chicago	17	21	20	30	11	–	99
New York	25	18	19	26	14	–	102

Technical fouls: Chicago 1 (Rodman, 2:03 lst). New York 1 (Oakley, 0:33 2nd). **Flagrant fouls:** None. **A:** 19,763. **T:** 3:02. **Officials:** Ed T Rush, Hue Hollins, Joe Derosa.

Game Four

CHICAGO (94)

	min	fg m–a	ft m–a	rb o–t	a	pf	tp
Rodman	41	3–10	0–2	10–19	3	5	6
Pippen	39	3–11	2–4	4–7	5	3	9
Longley	21	2–5	1–2	3–4	3	6	5
Jordan	40	7–23	11–13	2–8	8	5	27
Harper	40	6–15	3–3	3–5	2	2	18
Kerr	23	2–2	3–3	0–0	0	1	7
Brown	12	3–4	2–2	0–1	0	1	8
Edwards	4	1–4	0–0	0–0	0	2	2
Buechler	5	3–3	0–0	0–0	0	2	6
Wennington	7	2–3	0–0	0–0	1	1	4
Salley	8	1–1	0–0	1–2	0	0	2
Kukoc	DNP—back injury						
TOTALS	**240**	**33–81**	**22–29**	**23–46**	**22**	**28**	**94**

Percentages: FG–.407, FT–.759. **3-Point goals:** 6–20, .300 (Pippen 1–4, Jordan 2–7, Harper 3–9). **Team rebounds:** 9. **Blocked shots:** 6 (Longley 3, Rodman, Jordan, Brown). **Turnovers:** 17 (Rodman 6, Longley 3, Pippen 3, Harper 2, Brown). **Steals:** 7 (Jordan 2, Pippen 2, Rodman 2, Kerr).

NEW YORK (91)

	min	fg m–a	ft m–a	rb o–t	a	pf	tp
Oakley	38	6–9	5–6	3–5	0	5	17
Mason	38	0–2	1–2	0–5	3	4	1
Ewing	42	10–21	9–10	0–10	1	5	29
Starks	39	4–11	4–5	0–3	3	3	13
Harper	37	5–8	2–2	0–3	5	4	15
Ward	9	1–2	1–3	0–1	1	1	3
Anderson	14	1–1	2–2	0–1	0	3	5
Williams	4	0–0	0–0	0–0	0	2	0
Davis	19	2–4	4–4	1–1	1	0	8
Grandison	DNP—coach's decision						
Grant	DNP—coach's decision						
Reid	DNP—coach's decision						
TOTALS	**240**	**29–58**	**28–34**	**4–28**	**14**	**27**	**91**

Percentages: FG–.500, FT–.824. **3-Point goals:** 5–14, .357 (Oakley 0–1, Starks 1–5, Harper 3–6, Ward 0–1, Anderson 1–1). **Team rebounds:** 7. **Blocked shots:** 5 (Ewing 4, Williams). **Turnovers:** 20 (Starks 5, Ewing 4, Mason 4, Oakley 3, Anderson 2, Ward, Williams). **Steals:** 7 (Oakley 3, Starks 2, Harper, Ward).

Chicago	24	27	26	17	–	94
New York	28	22	18	23	–	91

Technical fouls: Chicago 3 (Rodman, 9:37 lst; Head Coach Jackson, 11:38 4th; Longley, 8:42 4th). New York 2 (Illegal Defense, 9:11 3rd; Oakley, 11:29 4th). **Flagrant fouls:** Chicago 1 (Jordan, 8:07 3rd). **A:** 19,763. **T:** 2:49. **Officials:** Mike Mathis, Bill Oakes, Ed Middleton.

NEW YORK (81)

	min	fg m–a	ft m–a	rb o–t	a	pf	tp
Oakley	41	5–8	4–7	3–13	2	4	14
Mason	41	6–8	4–7	1–6	2	3	16
Ewing	38	7–14	8–11	1–7	1	4	22
Starks	32	3–10	3–5	0–1	0	3	10
Harper	33	3–9	0–0	0–2	6	4	6
Anderson	22	3–9	0–0	1–5	1	3	6
Davis	17	2–4	0–0	0–0	0	1	4
Ward	15	1–4	0–0	0–2	3	1	3
Grandison	1	0–1	0–0	0–0	0	0	0
Grant	DNP—coach's decision						
Reid	DNP—coach's decision						
Williams	DNP—coach's decision						
TOTALS	240	30–67	19–30	6–36	15	23	81

Percentages: FG–.448, FT–.633. **3-Point goals:** 2–13, .154 (Starks 1–4, Harper 0–3, Anderson 0–1, Davis 0–1, Ward 1–3, Grandison 0–1). **Team rebounds:** 15. **Blocked shots:** 3 (Ewing 3). **Turnovers:** 20 (Ewing 5, Mason 4, Harper 3, Oakley 3, Starks 2, Anderson, Davis). **Steals:** 7 (Ward 4, Anderson 2, Oakley).

CHICAGO (94)

	min	fg m–a	ft m–a	rb o–t	a	pf	tp
Pippen	42	5–12	3–4	3–11	2	4	15
Rodman	31	5–9	1–2	4–12	3	6	11
Longley	23	1–7	2–2	1–3	1	6	4
Harper	36	4–7	3–4	1–5	5	1	12
Jordan	43	13–29	8–9	1–2	5	5	35
Wennington	24	2–7	0–0	1–4	3	3	4
Kerr	17	1–1	2–2	0–1	2	0	4
Buechler	5	2–4	0–0	0–0	0	0	5
Brown	13	1–2	2–2	2–5	1	1	4
Salley	6	0–0	0–0	0–0	1	2	0
Edwards	DNP—coach's decision						
Kukoc	DNP—back injury						
TOTALS	240	34–78	21–25	13–43	23	28	94

Percentages: FG–.436, FT–.840. **3-Point goals:** 5–11, .455 (Pippen 2–4, Harper 1–2, Jordan 1–2, Wennington 0–1, Buechler 1–2). **Team rebounds:** 2. **Blocked shots:** 2 (Longley, Wennington). **Turnovers:** 12 (Longley 3, Brown 2, Jordan 2, Buechler, Kerr, Pippen, Rodman, Wennington). **Steals:** 9 (Pippen 5, Harper 2, Jordan 2).

New York	18	18	23	22	–	81
Chicago	18	24	26	26	–	94

Technical fouls: New York 2 (Ewing, 6:03 lst; Harper, 8:28 3rd). Chicago 2 (Rodman 2 (ejected), 6:55 3rd, 1:29 4th). **Flagrant fouls:** None. **A:** 24,396. **T:** 2:30. **Officials:** Dick Bavetta, Steve Javie, Ronnie Nunn.

Heat Series

Three And Out!
Bulls Too Hot For The
Young Heat

Opening Round:
Miami Heat
(3–0)

Game 1 in Chicago (W): 102–85
Game 2 in Chicago (W): 106–75
Game 3 at Miami (W): 112–91

Count the Heat players trying to deny MJ. All Miami coach Pat Riley could do was stick all five of his players on Michael—and they still weren't enough.

The Worm rips the ball away from a stunned Alonzo Mourning.

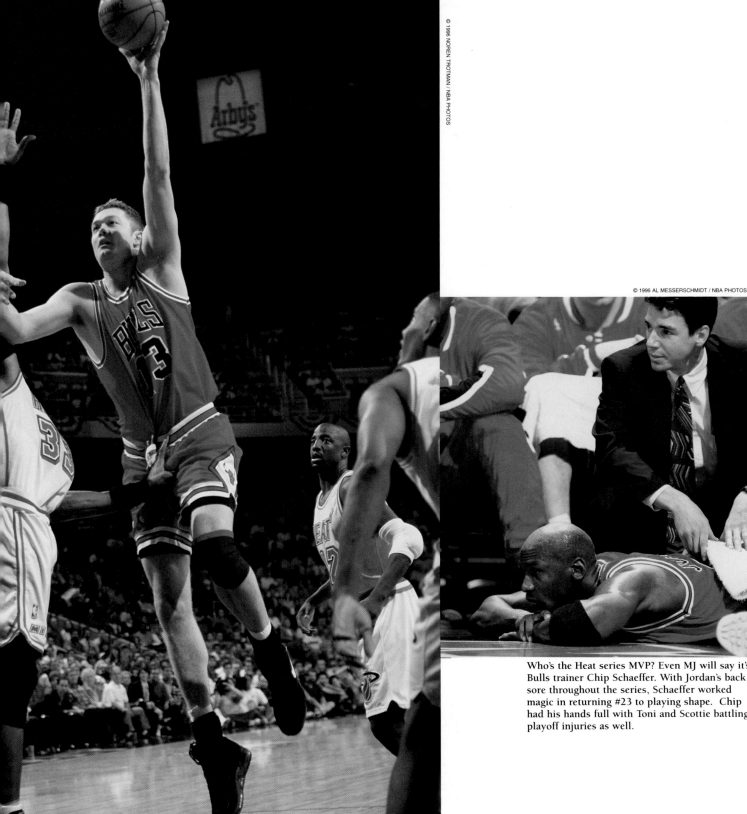

Who's the Heat series MVP? Even MJ will say it's Bulls trainer Chip Schaeffer. With Jordan's back sore throughout the series, Schaeffer worked magic in returning #23 to playing shape. Chip had his hands full with Toni and Scottie battling playoff injuries as well.

Luc Longley drives past Alonzo Mourning in game three. Luc struggled with foul trouble throughout the Heat series and the rest of the playoffs, but still proved valuable in battling the league's best centers.

His dangerous three-point shot on leave, Toni Kukoc floats past the Heat's Tim Hardaway for a lay-up. Having gone 1 for 16 from downtown, Kukoc adjusted his inside game to help sweep Miami.

In what has become a postgame United Center tradition, Dennis Rodman scans the crowd before tossing his jersey to a lucky recipient. In game two of the Heat series, the shirt tossing came a little early when Dennis himself was tossed after his second technical for rough-housing Alonzo Mourning.

An unsung hero throughout the series, Ron Harper celebrates the Bulls first playoff victory.

MIAMI (85)

	min	fg m–a	ft m–a	rb o–t	a	pf	tp
Thomas	26	2–4	2–2	1–6	1	6	6
Williams	34	5–11	1–2	1–8	1	1	12
Mourning	21	3–8	4–6	0–2	0	6	10
Chapman	34	4–9	0–0	0–1	1	1	10
Hardaway	44	12–19	1–2	0–3	7	2	30
Gatling	26	4–8	2–3	5–9	0	6	10
Askins	10	0–3	0–0	2–3	1	2	0
Schayes	10	1–1	0–0	0–1	0	1	2
Smith	13	1–1	0–0	0–0	2	4	2
Danilovic	22	1–3	0–0	0–0	1	3	3
Corbin	DNP—coach's decision						
King	DNP—coach's decision						
TOTALS	**240**	**33–67**	**10–15**	**9–33**	**14**	**32**	**85**

Percentages: FG–.493, FT–.667. **3-Point goals:** 9–23, .391 (Williams 1–5, Chapman 2–5, Hardaway 5–10, Askins 0–1, Danilovic 1–2). **Team rebounds:** 6. **Blocked shots:** 2 (Thomas, Williams). **Turnovers:** 28 (Hardaway 9, Mourning 6, Gatling 5, Thomas 2, Williams 2, Askins, Schayes, Smith). **Steals:** 8 (Hardaway 3, Danilovic, Gatling, Smith, Thomas, Williams).

CHICAGO (102)

	min	fg m–a	ft m–a	rb o–t	a	pf	tp
Pippen	42	4–10	5–8	1–8	3	1	13
Kukoc	38	9–17	2–4	1–7	3	1	21
Longley	14	1–3	2–2	2–3	2	6	4
Harper	26	5–8	1–2	1–1	2	2	11
Jordan	38	13–22	9–12	2–4	2	5	35
Rodman	27	1–3	1–2	5–10	1	4	3
Kerr	27	1–3	5–6	0–1	3	1	8
Wennington	7	1–3	0–0	1–2	0	0	2
Brown	5	1–2	0–0	0–0	0	0	2
Buechler	7	1–3	0–0	0–0	0	0	3
Salley	9	0–0	0–0	0–1	1	4	0
Edwards	DNP—coach's decision						
TOTALS	**240**	**37–74**	**25–36**	**13–37**	**17**	**24**	**102**

Percentages: FG–.500, FT–.694. **3-Point goals:** 3–17, .176 (Pippen 0–3, Kukoc 1–7, Harper 0–1, Jordan 0–1, Kerr 1–3, Buechler 1–2). **Team rebounds:** 11. **Blocked shots:** 4 (Longley 2, Pippen, Jordan). **Turnovers:** 21 (Jordan 4, Harper 3, Kukoc 3, Longley 3, Pippen 3, Rodman 2, Salley). **Steals:** 14 (Pippen 5, Harper 4, Kerr 2, Brown, Jordan, Salley).

Miami	22	32	13	18	–	85
Chicago	29	25	25	23	–	102

Technical fouls: Miami 9 (Thomas, 8:53 1st; Assistant Coach McAdoo, 4:22 1st; Gatling 2 (ejected), 3:25 1st, 2:40 4th; Illegal Defense, 8:58 4th; Mourning 2 (ejected), 3:49 4th; Head Coach Riley 2 (ejected), 3:49 4th). Chicago 2 (Rodman, 4:22 1st; Head Coach Jackson, 1:10 2nd). **Flagrant fouls:** None. **A:** 24,104. **T:** 2:24. **Officials:** Luis Grillo, Steve Javie, Joe Forte.

MIAMI (75)

	min	fg m–a	ft m–a	rb o–t	a	pf	tp
Thomas	17	0–1	0–0	0–2	0	2	0
Williams	17	0–4	0–0	1–1	2	1	0
Mourning	30	3–8	8–14	1–8	2	4	14
Chapman	24	5–10	0–0	0–1	2	4	11
Hardaway	28	2–9	4–5	0–0	4	5	9
Corbin	26	1–3	3–4	1–3	0	2	5
Gatling	22	1–6	3–6	3–11	0	1	5
Smith	26	4–8	0–0	1–2	3	3	10
Danilovic	23	5–9	3–3	1–1	1	4	15
Askins	8	0–1	0–0	0–2	0	2	0
King	12	0–3	1–2	0–3	1	1	1
Schayes	7	2–3	1–2	2–3	0	0	5
TOTALS	**240**	**23–65**	**23–36**	**10–37**	**15**	**29**	**75**

Percentages: FG–.354, FT–.639. **3-Point goals:** 6–20, .300 (Williams 0–2, Chapman 1–5, Hardaway 1–4, Smith 2–4, Danilovic 2–4, Askins 0–1). **Team rebounds:** 9. **Blocked shots:** 1 (Mourning). **Turnovers:** 21 (Mourning 7, Danilovic 3, Gatling 2, Hardaway 2, Thomas 2, Corbin, Schayes, Smith, Williams). **Steals:** 6 (Chapman 2, Corbin, Mourning, Smith, Thomas).

CHICAGO (106)

	min	fg m–a	ft m–a	rb o–t	a	pf	tp
Pippen	35	10–14	1–4	2–8	8	1	24
Kukoc	37	4–12	0–0	2–7	4	3	8
Longley	15	3–6	1–2	2–5	1	5	7
Harper	29	3–5	0–4	3–6	6	3	6
Jordan	32	9–17	9–12	0–4	4	0	29
Rodman	14	0–1	2–4	0–5	2	4	2
Wennington	8	0–0	0–0	2–3	1	3	0
Buechler	13	1–2	0–0	0–2	1	2	3
Kerr	22	3–7	6–6	0–2	4	3	13
Brown	10	3–4	0–0	0–0	0	0	6
Salley	17	1–2	1–3	0–1	0	3	3
Edwards	8	2–3	1–2	0–2	0	2	5
TOTALS	**240**	**39–73**	**21–37**	**11–45**	**31**	**29**	**106**

Percentages: FG–.534, FT–.568. **3-Point goals:** 7–21, .333 (Pippen 3–6, Kukoc 0–6, Harper 0–1, Jordan 2–3, Buechler 1–1, Kerr 1–4). **Team rebounds:** 14. **Blocked shots:** 3 (Pippen, Kukoc, Salley). **Turnovers:** 15 (Harper 2, Kukoc 2, Longley 2, Pippen 2, Rodman 2, Salley 2, Edwards, Kerr). **Steals:** 9 (Harper 3, Pippen 3, Buechler, Jordan, Wennington).

Miami	19	19	19	18	–	75
Chicago	28	35	24	19	–	106

Technical fouls: Miami 1 (Hardaway, 4:49 1st). Chicago 2 (Rodman 2 (ejected), 1:21 2nd; 3:01 3rd). **Flagrant fouls:** None. **A:** 24,202. **T:** 2:33. **Officials:** Mike Mathis, Bill Oakes, Paul Mihalak.

CHICAGO (112)

	min	fg m–a	ft m–a	rb o–t	a	pf	tp
Kukoc	30	4–8	6–7	1–5	4	2	14
Pippen	39	6–12	8–11	8–18	10	3	22
Longley	21	4–8	2–2	2–5	1	2	10
Jordan	33	10–23	3–3	1–3	2	0	26
Harper	34	5–6	2–2	0–2	3	2	13
Rodman	18	3–4	0–0	2–3	3	4	6
Kerr	23	2–5	2–2	0–1	3	0	7
Brown	7	0–0	1–2	0–1	0	1	1
Buechler	14	3–7	0–0	1–4	0	1	7
Salley	8	0–2	0–0	0–2	0	1	0
Wennington	13	3–5	0–0	2–4	1	1	6
Edwards	DNP—coach's decision						
TOTALS	**240**	**40–80**	**24–29**	**17–48**	**27**	**17**	**112**

Percentages: FG–.500, FT–.828. **3-Point goals:** 8–20, .400 (Kukoc 0–3, Pippen 2–4, Jordan 3–6, Harper 1–1, Kerr 1–3 Buechler 1–3). **Team rebounds:** 3. **Blocked shots:** 3 (Pippen 3). **Turnovers:** 12 (Pippen 5, Buechler 2, Harper, Kerr, Kukoc, Longley, Wennington). **Steals:** 8 (Jordan 3, Wennington 2, Kerr, Kukoc, Pippen).

MIAMI (91)

	min	fg m–a	ft m–a	rb o–t	a	pf	tp
Williams	19	1–3	0–0	1–3	2	2	2
Thomas	17	2–5	2–2	3–8	2	5	6
Mourning	41	11–19	8–8	2–8	2	3	30
Chapman	30	3–9	0–0	0–4	2	1	6
Hardaway	38	6–15	0–0	1–2	6	3	14
Gatling	20	1–8	1–3	2–4	1	1	3
Askins	30	4–7	3–3	1–3	1	5	13
Smith	22	4–10	0–0	2–2	3	0	10
Danilovic	15	3–6	0–0	0–0	2	1	7
Corbin	8	0–2	0–0	3–4	1	1	0
King	DNP—coach's decision						
Schayes	DNP—fractures right side of face						
TOTALS	**240**	**35–84**	**14–16**	**15–38**	**22**	**22**	**91**

Percentages: FG–.417, FT–.875. **3-Point goals:** 7–27, .259 (Williams 0–2, Chapman 0–3, Hardaway 2–8, Askins 2–4, Smith 2–6, Danilovic 1–4). **Team rebounds:** 7. **Blocked shots:** 2 (Mourning 2). **Turnovers:** 14 (Hardaway 4, Askins 3, Mourning 3, Chapman, Gatling, Smith, Thomas). **Steals:** 7 (Smith 2, Askins, Chapman, Corbin, Gatling, Mourning).

Chicago	37	25	27	23	–	112
Miami	23	21	22	25	–	91

Technical fouls: Miami 1 (Hardaway, 4:15 3rd). **Flagrant fouls:** None. **A:** 15,200. **T:** 2:12. **Officials:** Dick Bavetta, Bennett Salvatore, Ron Olesiak.

Regular Season

Regular Season Highlights (72–10)
Best Record In NBA History

Talk about a home court advantage —the Bulls set the NBA's record
for most consecutive home games won in the regular season with 44.

The league's most dominating
player on his way to a remarkable
eighth scoring title. He averaged
30.4 points per game.

General Manager Jerry Krause (left), NBA executive of the year, talks shop with Flip Saunders, head coach of the Minnesota Timberwolves.

Rodman battles the Phoenix phenom, Charles Barkley, under the basket.

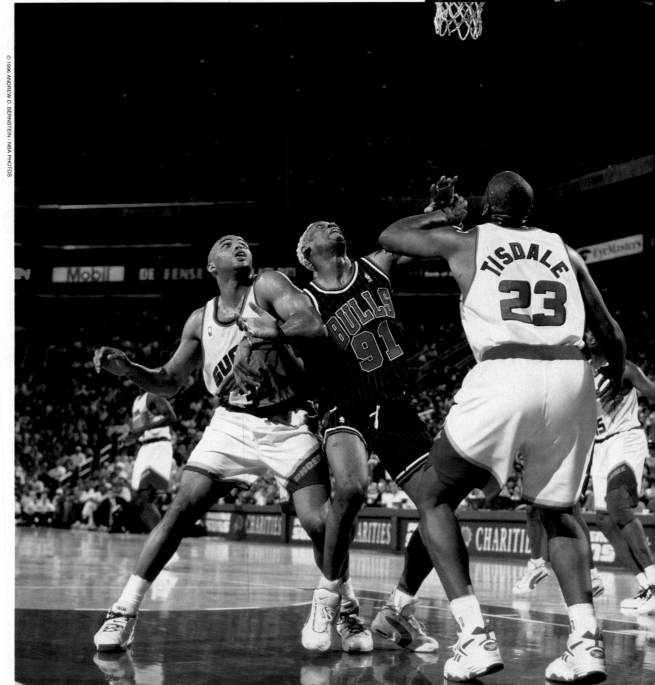

Hakeem Olajuwan and Clyde Drexler can do nothing but get out of Michael's way.

Toni Kukoc, the Waiter, looks to serve up an outlet pass
on to his way to the NBA's Sixth Man Award.

Steve Kerr, the NBA's all-time three-point field goal percentage leader, works free of the Washington Bullets' Brent Price for a jumper.

Pippen drives the ball home against Houston.

Rodman takes on Joe Smith while the Bulls visit Golden State.

Former arch-rivals...now teammates.

A restless Jackson
patrols the sidelines.

"Hey Hollins, give me a break!"

Phil's unheralded think-tank, (from left) assistant coaches Jim Cleamons (new head coach of the Mavericks), Jimmy Rodgers, and Tex Winter. Not shown: John Paxson, the Bulls advance scout.

the Ultimate Coach for the Ultimate Season

© 1996 SCOTT CUNNINGHAM / NBA PHOTOS

© 1996 ANDREW D. BERNSTEIN / NBA PHOTOS

Jackson said coaching no. 23 is "like coaching Michelangelo." Could Jackson and Michelangelo be discussing their impending, intertwined contract negotiations?

The coach with the best regular-season record in NBA history permits himself a small smile.

© 1996 SCOTT CUNNINGHAM / NBA PHOTOS

After seven years, three NBA championships, and more than 400 victories, Phil Jackson was finally recognized. He is the 1996 Coach of the Year. On the road to the best record in league history, a laid-back Coach Jackson used his unorthodox coaching methods to unite the many personalities of the Bulls into the greatest NBA team in history.

During the playoffs, Jackson matched wits with his long-time foe, the Heat's Pat Riley, with a young and brash coach with a promising future, Jeff Van Gundy of the Knicks, with an under-manned Brian Hill in Orlando, and with an equally defensive-minded George Karl of Seattle. When it counted, Jackson and his coaching staff made second-half adjustments that turned many games around.

Coaching the best rebounder of the 1990s, Dennis Rodman, a perennial all-star, Scottie Pippen, the top sixth man in the NBA, Toni Kukoc, and the best player in history, Michael Jordan—it can be said Chicago's Zen master has been afforded many luxuries the rest of the league simply can't match. But only Phil Jackson could have brought this group together and forged a team for all ages.

Ron Harper finishes a fast-break against Seattle's Shawn Kemp. Harper fought off a knee injury that sidelined him for much of games four and five to play a hero's role in the final game of the series.

Player Profiles

Randy Brown

POSITION: Guard
HEIGHT/WEIGHT: 6-2/191
BIRTHDATE: May 22, 1968, in Chicago, IL
COLLEGE: New Mexico State '91
NBA EXPERIENCE: 6 years
HOW RANDY BECAME A BULL: Signed as a free agent on October 5, 1995.

Jud Buechler

POSITION: Forward/Guard
HEIGHT/WEIGHT: 6-6/228
BIRTHDATE: June 19, 1968, in San Diego, CA
COLLEGE: Arizona '90
NBA EXPERIENCE: 6 years
HOW JUD BECAME A BULL: Signed as a free agent on September 29, 1994.

Jason Caffey

POSITION: Forward
HEIGHT/WEIGHT: 6-8/255
BIRTHDATE: June 12, 1973, in Mobile, AL
COLLEGE: Alabama '95
NBA EXPERIENCE: Rookie
HOW JASON BECAME A BULL: Selected by Chicago in the first round
(20th overall) of the 1995 NBA Draft.

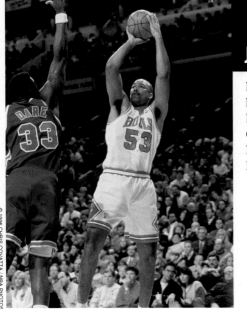

James Edwards

POSITION: Center
HEIGHT/WEIGHT: 7-1/252
BIRTHDATE: November 22, 1955, in Seattle, WA
COLLEGE: Washington '77
NBA EXPERIENCE: 19 years
HOW JAMES BECAME A BULL: Signed as a free agent on October 26, 1995.

Jack Haley

POSITION: Center/Forward
HEIGHT/WEIGHT: 6-10/258
BIRTHDATE: January 27, 1964
COLLEGE: UCLA '87
NBA EXPERIENCE: 8 years
HOW JACK BECAME A BULL: Signed as a free agent.

Ron Harper

POSITION: Guard
HEIGHT/WEIGHT: 6-6/216
BIRTHDATE: January 20, 1964, in Dayton, OH
COLLEGE: Miami-Ohio '86
NBA EXPERIENCE: 10 years
HOW RON BECAME A BULL: Signed as a free agent on September 19, 1994.

Michael Jordan

POSITION: Guard
HEIGHT/WEIGHT: 6-6/216
BIRTHDATE: February 17, 1963, in Brooklyn, NY
COLLEGE: North Carolina '85
NBA EXPERIENCE: 11 years
HOW MICHAEL BECAME A BULL: Selected by Chicago in the first round
(third overall) of the 1984 NBA Draft.

Steve Kerr

POSITION: Guard
HEIGHT/WEIGHT: 6-3/181
BIRTHDATE: September 27, 1965, in Beirut, Lebanon
COLLEGE: Arizona '88
NBA EXPERIENCE: 8 years
HOW STEVE BECAME A BULL: Signed as a free agent on September 29, 1993.

Toni Kukoc

POSITION: Forward/Guard
HEIGHT/WEIGHT: 6-11/232
BIRTHDATE: September 18, 1968, in Split, Croatia
NBA EXPERIENCE: 3 years
HOW TONI BECAME A BULL: Selected by Chicago in the second round
(29th overall) of the 1990 NBA Draft.

Luc Longley

POSITION: Center
HEIGHT/WEIGHT: 7-2/292
BIRTHDATE: January 19, 1969, in Melbourne, Australia
COLLEGE: New Mexico '91
NBA EXPERIENCE: 5 years
HOW LUC BECAME A BULL: Acquired in a trade from Minnesota for Stacey King on February 23, 1994.

Scottie Pippen

POSITION: Forward/Guard
HEIGHT/WEIGHT: 6-7/228
BIRTHDATE: September 25, 1965, in Hamburg, AR
COLLEGE: Central Arkansas '87
NBA EXPERIENCE: 9 years
HOW SCOTTIE BECAME A BULL: Draft rights traded by SuperSonics to Chicago for draft rights to Olden Polynice, a 1988 or 1989 draft choice and option to exchange 1989 first round draft choices on June 22, 1987.

Dennis Rodman

POSITION: Forward
HEIGHT/WEIGHT: 6-6/220
BIRTHDATE: MAY 13, 1961, in Trenton, NJ
COLLEGE: Southeastern Oklahoma State '86
NBA EXPERIENCE: 10 years
HOW DENNIS BECAME A BULL: Acquired in a trade from San Antonio for Will Perdue on October 2, 1995.

John Salley

POSITION: Center
HEIGHT/WEIGHT: 6-11/255
BIRTHDATE: June 16, 1964, in Brooklyn, NY
COLLEGE: Georgia Tech '86
NBA EXPERIENCE: 10 years
HOW JOHN BECAME A BULL: Signed 10-day contract on 3/4... Signed second
   10-day contract on 3/14... Signed for the remainder of the season on 3/23.

Dickey Simpkins

POSITION: Forward
HEIGHT/WEIGHT: 6-9/248
BIRTHDATE: April 6, 1972, in Washington, DC
COLLEGE: Providence '94
NBA EXPERIENCE: 2 years
HOW DICKEY BECAME A BULL: Selected by Chicago in the first round
   (21st overall) of the 1994 NBA Draft.

Bill Wennington

POSITION: Center
HEIGHT/WEIGHT: 7-0/277
BIRTHDATE: April 26, 1963, in Montreal, Canada
COLLEGE: St. John's University '85
NBA EXPERIENCE: 9 years
HOW JOHN BECAME A BULL: Signed as a free agent on September 29, 1993.

Chicago Bulls

Regular Season Statistics
(72–10)

PLAYER	G	GS	MIN	Field Goals			3 Point FG			Free Throws		
				FG	FGA	PCT	FG	FGA	PCT	FT	FTA	PCT
Jordan	82	82	3090	916	1850	.495	111	260	.427	548	657	.834
Pippen	77	77	2825	563	1216	.463	150	401	.374	220	324	.679
Kukoc	81	20	2103	386	787	.490	87	216	.403	206	267	.772
Longley	62	62	1641	242	502	.482	0	0	—	80	103	.777
Kerr	82	0	1919	244	482	.506	122	237	.515	78	84	.929
Harper	80	80	1886	234	501	.467	28	104	.269	98	139	.705
Rodman	64	57	2088	146	304	.480	3	27	.111	56	106	.528
Wennington	71	20	1065	169	343	.493	1	1	1.000	37	43	.860
Haley	1	0	7	2	6	.333	0	0	—	1	2	.500
Salley (TOT)	42	6	673	63	140	.450	0	0	—	59	85	.694
Salley (CHI)	17	0	191	12	35	.343	0	0	—	12	20	.600
Buechler	74	0	740	112	242	.463	40	90	.444	14	22	.636
Simpkins	60	12	685	77	160	.481	1	1	1.000	61	97	.629
Edwards	28	0	274	41	110	.373	0	0	—	16	26	.615
Caffey	57	0	545	71	162	.438	0	1	.000	40	68	.588
Brown	68	0	671	78	192	.406	1	11	.091	28	46	.609
BULLS	82		19730	3293	6892	.478	544	1349	.403	1495	2004	.746
OPPONENTS	82		19730	2880	6428	.448	437	1249	.350	1424	1985	.717

PLAYER	Rebounds			AST	PF	DQ	STL	TO	BLK	PTS	AVG
	OFF	DEF	TOT								
Jordan	148	395	543	352	195	0	180	197	42	2491	30.4
Pippen	152	344	496	452	198	0	133	207	57	1496	19.4
Kukoc	115	208	323	287	150	0	64	114	28	1065	13.1
Longley	104	214	318	119	223	4	22	114	84	564	9.1
Kerr	25	85	110	192	109	0	63	42	2	688	8.4
Harper	74	139	213	208	137	0	105	73	32	594	7.4
Rodman	356	596	952	160	196	1	36	138	27	351	5.5
Wennington	58	116	174	46	171	1	21	37	16	376	5.3
Haley	1	1	2	0	2	0	0	1	0	5	5.0
Salley (TOT)	46	94	140	54	110	3	19	55	27	185	4.4
Salley (CHI)	20	23	43	15	38	0	8	16	15	36	2.1
Buechler	45	66	111	56	70	0	34	39	7	278	3.8
Simpkins	66	90	156	38	78	0	9	56	8	216	3.6
Edwards	15	25	40	11	61	1	1	21	8	98	3.5
Caffey	51	60	111	24	91	3	12	48	7	182	3.2
Brown	17	49	66	73	88	0	57	31	12	185	2.7
BULLS	1247	2411	3658	2033	1807	10	745	1175	345	8625	105.2
OPPONENTS	981	2136	3117	1592	1856	25	595	1405	312	7621	92.9

Regular Season Statistics
(72–10)

Single-Game Highs · Average Per Game

PLAYER	MIN	REB	AST	ST	TO	BL	PTS	MIN	REB	AST	STL	TO	BLK	PTS
Jordan	49	16	8	6	8	3	53	37.7	6.6	4.3	2.20	2.4	0.51	30.4
Pippen	49	13	14	5	12	5	40	36.7	6.4	5.9	1.73	2.7	0.74	19.4
Kukoc	42	10	11	5	5	2	34	26.0	4.0	3.5	0.79	1.4	0.35	13.1
Longley	37	11	5	3	5	7	21	26.5	5.1	1.9	0.35	1.8	1.35	9.1
Kerr	32	5	6	6	4	1	19	23.4	1.3	2.3	0.77	0.5	0.02	8.4
Harper	39	8	7	4	4	3	22	23.6	2.7	2.6	1.31	0.9	0.40	7.4
Rodman	44	24	10	3	4	2	12	32.6	14.9	2.5	0.56	2.2	0.42	5.5
Wennington	35	11	5	3	3	2	18	15.0	2.5	0.6	0.30	0.5	0.23	5.3
Haley	7	2	0	0	1	0	5	7.0	2.0	0.0	0.00	1.0	0.00	5.0
Salley (TOT)	32	12	5	2	4	4	15	16.0	3.3	1.3	0.45	1.3	0.64	4.4
Salley (CHI)	19	8	3	2	3	3	12	11.2	2.5	0.9	0.47	0.9	0.88	2.1
Buechler	30	6	4	2	3	1	14	10.0	1.5	0.8	0.46	0.5	0.09	3.8
Simpkins	25	8	4	1	4	1	12	11.4	2.6	0.6	0.15	0.9	0.13	3.6
Edwards	23	5	2	1	3	2	12	9.8	1.4	0.4	0.04	0.8	0.29	3.5
Caffey	24	8	2	2	4	1	13	9.6	1.9	0.4	0.21	0.8	0.12	3.2
Brown	27	3	6	6	4	1	16	9.9	1.0	1.1	0.84	0.5	0.18	2.7
BULLS	265	57	38	14	23	14	127	240.6	44.6	24.8	9.09	14.3	4.21	105.2
OPPONENTS	265	66	30	14	26	10	114	240.6	38.0	19.4	7.26	17.1	3.80	92.9

Career Highs (C = Set, T = Tied This Season)

PLAYER	FG	FGA	FT	FTA	REB	AST	PTS
Jordan	27	49	26	27	18	17	69
Pippen	18	34	12	21	18	15	43
Kukoc	13	21T	11C	13	13	11T	34C
Longley	9C	16	7T	9C	19	8	21C
Kerr	9	16	7	9	6	11	24
Harper	19	31	16	20	16	15	40
Rodman	15	21	9	12	34	10C	34
Wennington	9T	21C	8	8	14	5T	21
Haley	8	16	7	11	18	3	19
Salley (TOT)	10	18	11	12	17	8	28
Salley (CHI)							
Buechler	8	16	5	9	9	4T	19
Simpkins	6	11	7	8T	10	4T	16
Edwards	16	29	18	19	18	7	39
Caffey	5C	11C	6C	10C	8C	2C	13C
Brown	10	15	6	8	10	8	27
BULLS	67	122	56	71	82	52	156
OPPONENTS	64	118	48	60	66C	47	155

Chicago Bulls '95–'96

Game by Game

Game	Date	Opponent*	W/L	Score	Record	High Scorer /Rebounder /Assists
1	11/03	Hornets	W	105–91	1–0	Jordan 42, Rodman 11, Jordan 7
2	11/04	Celtics	W	107–85	2–0	Pippen 21, Rodman 8, Pippen 5
3	11/07	Raptors	W	117–108	3–0	Jordan 38, Rodman 13, Pippen 8
4	11/09	Cleveland	W	106–88	4–0	Jordan 29, Pippen 13, Pippen 12
5	11/11	Trailblazers	W	110–106	5–0	Jordan 36, Pippen 9, Jordan 7
6	11/14	Orlando	L	88–94	5–1	Jordan 23, Pippen 10, Pippen 6
7	11/15	Cavaliers	W	113–94	6–1	Pippen 27, Caffey 8, Pippen 8
8	11/17	Nets	W	109–94	7–1	Kukoc 19, Longley 8, Kukoc 7
9	11/21	Dallas	W	108–102	8–1	Jordan 36, Pippen 12, Pippen 7
10	11/22	San Antonio	W	103–94	9–1	Jordan 38, Longley 11, Pippen 13
11	11/24	Utah	W	90–85	10–1	Jordan 34, Longley 10, Jordan 6
12	11/26	Seattle	L	92–97	10–2	Jordan 22, Pippen 12, Pippen 5
13	11/27	Portland	W	107–104	11–2	Jordan 33, Wennington 5, Pippen 10
14	11/30	Vancouver	W	94–88	12–2	Jordan 29, Longley 10, Pippen 8
15	12/02	L.A. Clippers	W	104–98	13–2	Jordan 37, Pippen 13, Pippen 6
16	12/06	Knicks	W	101–94	14–2	Pippen 22, Rodman 20, Pippen 8
17	12/08	Spurs	W	106–87	15–2	Jordan 28, Rodman 21, Jordan 6
18	12/09	Milwaukee	W	118–106	16–2	Jordan 45, Rodman 21, Pippen 6
19	12/13	Magic	W	112–103	17–2	Jordan 36, Rodman 19, Pippen 6
20	12/14	Atlanta	W	127–108	18–2	Pippen 30, Rodman 10, Pippen 8
21	12/16	Lakers	W	108–88	19–2	Pippen 33, Rodman 15, Pippen 6
22	12/18	Boston	W	123–114	20–2	Pippen 37, Rodman 17, Pippen 12
23	12/19	Mavericks	W	114–101	21–2	Jordan 32, Rodman 13, Kerr 6
24	12/22	Raptors	W	113–104	22–2	Jordan 27, Jordan 10, Jordan 5
25	12/23	Jazz	W	100–86	23–2	Jordan 30, Rodman 12, Jordan 8
26	12/26	Indiana	L	97–103	23–3	Jordan 30, Rodman 11, Pippen 6
27	12/29	Pacers	W	120–93	24–3	Jordan 29, Rodman 16, Pippen 8
28	12/30	Hawks	W	95–93	25–3	Jordan 33, Rodman 21, Jordan 6
29	01/03	Rockets	W	100–86	26–3	Jordan 38, Rodman 15, Pippen 9
30	01/04	Charlotte	W	117–93	27–3	Jordan 27, Rodman 11, Harper 7
31	01/06	Bucks	W	113–84	28–3	Jordan 32, Rodman 16, Pippen 6
32	01/10	Sonics	W	113–87	29–3	Jordan 35, Jordan 14, Pippen 5
33	01/13	Philadelphia	W	120–93	30–3	Jordan 48, Rodman 16, Pippen 10
34	01/15	Washington	W	116–109	31–3	Jordan 46, Rodman 15, Pippen 6
35	01/16	76ers	W	116–104	32–3	Jordan 32, Rodman 21, Rodman 10
36	01/18	Toronto	W	92–89	33–3	Jordan 38, Rodman 13, Rodman 4
37	01/21	Detroit	W	111–96	34–3	Jordan 36, Rodman 9, Pippen 6
38	01/23	New York	W	99–79	35–3	Jordan 33, Rodman 13, Pippen 6
39	01/24	Grizzlies	W	104–84	36–3	Pippen 30, Rodman 16, Harper 7
40	01/26	Heat	W	102–80	37–3	Jordan 25, Rodman 16, Rodman 5
41	01/28	Suns	W	93–82	38–3	Jordan 31, Rodman 20, Jordan 6
42	01/30	Houston	W	98–87	39–3	Pippen 28, Pippen 12, Pippen 5
43	02/01	Sacramento	W	105–85	40–3	Jordan 27, Rodman 21, Kukoc 5
44	02/02	L.A. Lakers	W	99–84	41–3	Pippen 30, Rodman 23, Jordan 7
45	02/04	Denver	L	99–105	41–4	Jordan 39, Rodman 12, Wennington 5
46	02/06	Phoenix	L	96–106	41–5	Jordan 28, Rodman 14, Pippen 8
47	02/07	Golden State	W	99–95	42–5	Jordan 40, Rodman 18, Jordan 6
48	02/13	Bullets	W	111–98	43–5	Jordan 32, Rodman 16, Pippen 4
49	02/15	Detroit	W	112–109	44–5	Jordan 32, Rodman 19, Pippen 6
50	02/16	Minnesota	W	103–100	45–5	Jordan 35, Rodman 19, Pippen 7
51	02/18	Indiana	W	110–102	46–5	Jordan 44, Rodman 23, Jordan 7
52	02/20	Cavaliers	W	102–76	47–5	Harper 22, Rodman 15, Pippen 8
53	02/22	Atlanta	W	96–91	48–5	Jordan 34, Rodman 20, Pippen 10
54	02/23	Miami	L	104–113	48–6	Jordan 31, Rodman 11, Pippen 6

*Home games=opponent's team name; away games=opponent's city/state

Continued

Game	Date	Opponent	W/L	Score	Record	High Scorer /Rebounder /Assists
55	02/25	Magic	W	111–91	49–6	Kukoc 24, Rodman 17, Jordan 7
56	02/27	Timberwolves	W	120–99	50–6	Jordan 35, Rodman 24, Jordan 7
57	03/01	Warriors	W	110–87	51–6	Pippen 25, Rodman 17, Jordan 6
58	03/02	Celtics	W	107–75	52–6	Jordan 21, Rodman 15, Jordan 8
59	03/05	Bucks	W	115–106	53–6	Jordan 33, Rodman 9, Kukoc 7
60	03/07	Pistons	W	102–81	54–6	Jordan 53, Rodman 13, Pippen 10
61	03/10	New York	L	72–104	54–7	Jordan 32, Rodman 10, Pippen 5
62	03/13	Bullets	W	103–86	55–7	Jordan 37, Rodman 14, Jordan 5
63	03/15	Nuggets	W	108–87	56–7	Jordan 33, Rodman 15, Kukoc 10
64	03/16	New Jersey	W	97–93	57–7	Jordan 37, Jordan 16, Jordan 5
65	03/18	Philadelphia	W	98–94	58–7	Jordan 38, Jordan 11, Kukoc 11
66	03/19	Kings	W	89–67	59–7	Jordan 20, Jordan 9, Kukoc 7
67	03/21	Knicks	W	107–86	60–7	Jordan 36, Jordan 11, Kukoc 5
68	03/24	Toronto	L	108–109	60–8	Jordan 36, Pippen 9, Pippen 6
69	03/28	Hawks	W	111–80	61–8	Kukoc 24, Pippen 11, Pippen 8
70	03/30	Clippers	W	106–85	62–8	Pippen 22, Kukoc 9, Jordan 6
71	04/02	Miami	W	110–92	63–8	Pippen 32, Rodman 13, Harper 6
72	04/04	Heat	W	100–92	64–8	Jordan 40, Rodman 12, Pippen 8
73	04/05	Charlotte	W	126–92	65–8	Pippen 28, Rodman 17, Pippen 14
74	04/07	Orlando	W	90–86	66–8	Jordan 27, Rodman 13, Pippen 5
75	04/08	Hornets	L	97–98	66–9	Jordan 40, Rodman 17, Pippen 6
76	04/11	New Jersey	W	113–100	67–9	Jordan 17, Rodman 12, Kukoc 6
77	04/12	76ers	W	112–82	68–9	Jordan 23, Rodman 16, Pippen 6
78	04/14	Cleveland	W	98–72	69–9	Jordan 32, Jordan 12, Kukoc 5
79	**04/16**	**Milwaukee**	**W**	**86–80**	**70–9**	**Jordan 22, Rodman 19, Rodman 4**
80	04/18	Pistons	W	110–79	71–9	Jordan 30, Rodman 18, Pippen 8
81	04/20	Pacers	L	99–100	71–10	Jordan 24, Rodman 15, Jordan 6
82	04/21	Washington	W	103–93	72–10	Jordan 26, Rodman 11, Pippen 5

Playoffs

1	04/26	Heat	W	102–85	1–0	Jordan 35, Rodman 10, Three players 3
2	04/28	Heat	W	106–75	2–0	Jordan 29, Pippen 8, Pippen 8
3	05/01	Miami	W	112–91	**3–0**	Jordan 26, Pippen18, Pippen 10
1	05/05	Knicks	W	91–84	1–0	Jordan 44, Rodman 12, Pippen 7
2	05/07	Knicks	W	91–80	2–0	Jordan 28, Rodman 19, Pippen 6
3	05/11	New York	L	99–102	2–1	Jordan 46, Rodman 16, Pippen 6
4	05/12	New York	W	94–91	3–1	Jordan 27, Rodman 19, Jordan 8
5	05/14	Knicks	W	94–81	**4–1**	Jordan 35, Rodman 12, Harper 5
1	05/19	Magic	W	121–83	1–0	Jordan 21, Rodman 21, Kukoc 10
2	05/19	Magic	W	93–88	2–0	Jordan 35, Rodman 12, Pippen 9
3	05/25	Orlando	W	86–67	3–0	Pippen 27, Rodman 16, Pippen 7
4	05/27	Orlando	W	106–101	**4–0**	Jordan 45, Rodman 14, Pippen 8
1	06/05	Supersonics	W	107–90	1–0	Jordan 28, Rodman 13, Harper 7
2	06/07	Supersonics	W	92–88	2–0	Jordan 29, Rodman 20, Jordan 8
3	06/09	Seattle	W	108–86	3–0	Pippen 36, Rodman 10, Pippen 9
4	06/12	Seattle	L	86–107	3–1	Jordan 23, Rodman 14, Pippen 8
5	06/14	Seattle	L	78–89	3–2	Jordan 26, Rodman 12, Pippen 5
6	06/16	Supersonics	W	87–75	**4–2**	Jordan 22, Rodman 19, Jordan 7

Milestones

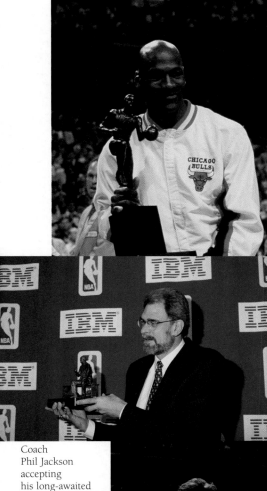

A beaming Michael Jordan adds the 1995–96 MVP Award to his trophy case.

Coach Phil Jackson accepting his long-awaited Coach of the Year trophy.

Make room for a newcomer. Toni Kukoc receives his Sixth Man Award.

- The Bulls continued their sellout streak in the second season at the United Center after moving from Chicago Stadium. The current sellout streak stands at 427 consecutive games—the second longest sellout streak in the NBA.

- Scottie Pippen recorded his 15th and 16th career triple-double this season on November 9 at Cleveland (18 points, 13 rebounds and 12 assists) and November 22 at San Antonio (15 points, 21 rebounds and 10 assists).

- Michael Jordan became the Bulls' all-time career leader in games played with 697 games on November 27 at Portland. Previously, Jerry Sloan held the record with 696 career games.

- Michael Jordan scored his 23,000th career point on January 13 at Philadelphia, scoring a game-high 48 points. He became one of only 13 players in the NBA to accumulate 23,000 career points.

- Dennis Rodman recorded his first career triple-double on January 16 at Philadelphia (10 pts, 21 rebounds and 10 assists).

- In January 1996, the Bulls went undefeated for the first time in any month of the club's 30-year history.

- In February, at Market Square Arena, Michael Jordan (44) and Scottie Pippen (40) became the first Chicago Bulls to score 40+ points in the same game.

- Michael Jordan scored his 24,000th career point on March 18 at Philadelphia and he became the 10th NBA player in League history to reach 24,000 points.

- Head Coach Phil Jackson reached his 400th career coaching victory, when the Bulls defeated the Sixers 98–94 on March 18. Jackson became the 26th coach in NBA history to do so and is one of 10 active coaches to accomplish this feat.

- Michael Jordan's 2,000th career steal came on April 4 vs. Miami and he became the fourth NBA player in history to reach 2,000 career steals.

- The Bulls 72–10 regular season wins break the record for most wins in NBA history.

- Michael Jordan is NBA scoring champ for the eighth time with 30.4 average per game.

- Dennis Rodman captures fifth consecutive rebounding title with 14.9 average.

- Steve Kerr, the NBA's all-time three-point field goal percentage leader (.480), finished second in the NBA in three-point field goal percentage at .515 (122–237).

- Bulls set the NBA's best record for most consecutive home games won in the regular season—44 and the NBA's record for most consecutive regular season home games won at the start of the season—37.

- Head Coach Phil Jackson wins NBA Coach of the Year honor.

- General Manager Jerry Krause earned the 1995–96 NBA Executive of the Year Award.

- Toni Kukoc voted NBA's top sixth man.

- Michael Jordan receives his fourth NBA Most Valuable Player trophy.

- Michael Jordan, Scottie Pippen and Dennis Rodman earn spots on the NBA All-Defense first team.

- Michael Jordan and Scottie Pippen voted members of All-NBA first team.